Methods
and
Data Analysis
for
Cross-Cultural
Research

Cross-Cultural Psychology Series

SERIES EDITORS

Walter J. Lonner
Western Washington University

John W. Berry
Queens University

Methods and Data Analysis for Cross-Cultural Research

Fons van de Vijver
Kwok Leung

CCP
Cross-Cultural Psychology

SAGE Publications
International Educational and Professional Publisher
Thousand Oaks   London   New Delhi

For information address:

SAGE Publications, Inc.
2455 Teller Road
Thousand Oaks, California 91320
E-mail: order@sagepub.com

SAGE Publications Ltd.
6 Bonhill Street
London EC2A 4PU
United Kingdom

SAGE Publications India Pvt. Ltd.
M-32 Market
Greater Kailash I
New Delhi 110 048 India

Printed in the United States of America

Library of Congress Cataloging-in-Publication Data

Vijver, Fons J. R. van de.
   Methods and data analysis for cross-cultural research / Fons J. R. van de Vijver, Kwok Leung.
      p.   cm. — (Cross-cultural psychology; vol. 1)
   Includes bibliographical references and index.
   ISBN 0-7619-0106-X. — ISBN 0-7619-0107-8 (pbk.)
   1. Ethnopsychology. I. Leung, Kwok, 1958-   . II. Title.
III. Series.
GN502.V55   1997
155.8′2—dc21   96-51274

97 98 99 00 01 02 03 10 9 8 7 6 5 4 3 2 1

Acquiring Editor:	Jim Nageotte
Editorial Assistant:	Kathleen Derby
Production Editor:	Astrid Virding
Production Assistant:	Karen Wiley
Typesetter/Designer:	Janelle LeMaster
Indexer:	Cristina Haley
Cover Designer:	Lesa Valdez
Print Buyer:	Anna Chin

Contents

Box List

Series Editors' Introduction

The comparative study of thought and behavior across cultures has been one of the most interesting and productive developments in psychology during the past quarter century. We believe, as do many others, that psychology can mature into a valid and global discipline only to the extent that it incorporates paradigms, perspectives, and data from an ever-widening circle of both cultures and ethnic groups. That was the general guiding philosophy behind the **Cross-Cultural Research and Methodology** series that was started in 1975, in which 20 volumes were published. Like the CCRM series, this new series offers books describing and critically examining Western-based psychology and its underlying assumptions. Most of the basic assumptions contained in standard psychology curricula in the many universities of the highly industrialized Western world have been unchallenged. The volumes in this new series present cultural elements that challenge Western ways of thinking in the hope of stimulating informed discussions about human behavior in all domains of psychology. Books in this series are written for use as core texts or as supplements, depending on the instructor's requirements. We believe that the cumulative totality of books in the series will contribute to the development of a much more inclusive psychology and will lead to the formation of interesting, testable hypotheses about the complex relationships between culture and behavior.

As series editors, we are fortunate to have an international panel of experts in cross-cultural psychology to help guide us in the selection and evaluation of manuscripts. The 14 members of the editorial board represent 11 different countries and many of the domains within psychology.

The first volume in this new series deals with what is probably the single most important concern in the comparative study of thought and behavior across cultures and ethnic groups: designing and conducting solid and informed research and analyzing data properly. Without a degree of sophistication in the development of hypotheses, using appropriate research strategies to test them, and analyzing data thoroughly and sensitively, research efforts can be at best misleading and at worst fatally flawed. Fons van de Vijver and Kwok Leung are among a handful of cross-cultural researchers who represent considerable insight and expertise in cross-cultural research. They are aware of the major issues and problems in this type of research, and they have been frequent contributors to the literature. We believe this book is a major contribution to the cross-cultural research literature and will be critically important to the development of future research and proper interpretation of data that are often gathered in unusual ways in places that are foreign to the researchers.

It is a pleasure for us to present this volume as the first in a series of books that will be important in the development of cross-cultural psychology, and indeed in related fields. Since research methods are typically generic and generalizable, researchers and scholars in a variety of fields will benefit from the skills and knowledge that van de Vijver and Leung impart in the book.

—Walter J. Lonner
—John W. Berry

Foreword

Cross-cultural research is burgeoning. Behavioral and social sciences such as psychology, sociology, management, marketing, and political science witness a steady increase of cross-cultural studies. For example, during the past decade there has been a consistently increasing number of psychological studies on cross-cultural similarities and differences (van de Vijver & Lonner, 1995). The increased interest is undoubtedly inspired by various factors, such as the opening of previously sealed international borders, large migration streams, the globalization of the economic market, international tourism, increased cross-cultural communications, and technological innovations such as new means of telecommunication.

The increase in the number of cross-cultural studies is not primarily due to an increase in the number of scientists who devote most or all of

AUTHORS' NOTE: Comments on an earlier version by John Adamopoulos, Richard Brislin, Barbara Byrne, Wai Chan, Todd Little, Robert McCrae, Ype Poortinga, Peter Smith, Harry Triandis, Yin-Fai Yung, and Zhang Jianxin are gratefully acknowledged.

their research to cross-cultural studies. Rather, cross-cultural research is for most researchers a natural extension of earlier, usually intracultural work. Cross-cultural research has various unique features. Researchers will have to deal with various methodological issues that they did not have to consider in intracultural research, such as the sampling of cultures and testing the accuracy of translations.

The present book can be seen as an extension and integration of previous work in methodological issues in cross-cultural research. The first, titled *Cross-Cultural Research Methods*, appeared in 1973 and was written by Brislin, Lonner, and Thorndike. The next was the volume on methodology in the six-volume *Handbook of Cross-Cultural Psychology* (Triandis & Berry, 1980), followed by Lonner and Berry's (1986) *Field Methods in Cross-Cultural Research*.

Most cross-cultural research in the past was largely monodisciplinary. More recently, however, there are more cross-disciplinary studies (see, e.g., Inkeles & Sasaki's, 1996, *Comparing Nations and Cultures*). From a methodological perspective this is an important development, because all cross-cultural researchers have to deal with a set of similar problems such as the (in)equality of the meaning of the phenomena that they study across cultural groups, the appropriateness of measurement instruments across cultures, and the accuracy of data collected to answer research questions and hypotheses.

Many methodological innovations have taken place in the past 25 years. Relevant new data-analytical tools have become available (such as item bias analysis and the analysis of covariance structures); as a consequence, the methodology for cross-cultural studies has become much more sophisticated in this period (e.g., quasi-experiments). Moreover, many empirical studies have provided useful insights about various methodological approaches and data analyses. An attempt is made to present the most important tools of cross-cultural research. The present book gives an up-to-date overview of methodological and data-analytical issues of cross-cultural studies.

Statistical techniques will not be described in detail, but we will focus on the relevance of methodological and statistical tools in cross-cultural research: What are the relevant research questions that can be tackled with a particular technique? The most important techniques are illustrated in boxes.

The book is meant for graduate students and professionals with an interest in cross-cultural studies. A basic knowledge of methodology and statistics and some sensitivity to issues in cross-cultural research are assumed; however, an advanced knowledge of statistics or cross-cultural research is not required.

1

Methodological Concepts in Cross-Cultural Research

Setting the Stage: Methodological Features of Cross-Cultural Studies

This book addresses methodological features of cross-cultural research. The common characteristic of such studies is their comparative nature, which involves the comparison of at least two cultural populations. Many studies involve different nation states, in sociology (e.g., Farberow, 1975; Ingelhart, 1977), education (Altbach, Arnove, & Kelly, 1982), the political sciences (e.g., Dogan & Pelassy, 1990; Rummel, 1972), management (e.g., Smith & Peterson, 1988), and psychology (e.g., Buss, 1989; Hofstede, 1980). Yet comparative studies can also involve different ethnic groups from a single country, such as the comparison of Blacks, Whites, and Hispanics in the United States (e.g., Schmidt & Hunter, 1977). In the cognitive domain such studies are more common than cross-national studies (van de Vijver, 1996).

Cross-Cultural Studies as Quasi-Experiments

Methodological aspects of experimental designs have been well documented (e.g., Campbell & Stanley, 1966). In so-called true experiments there are usually two groups. The experimental group is exposed to a treatment such as a drug or an educational curriculum that the control group does not receive. The treatment is called the independent variable, and the experimental and control groups have a different status on the independent variable. Ideally, the two groups differ only in the independent variable and are similar in all other respects ("all other things being equal"). The effect of the treatment on the outcome variable, the dependent variable, is usually evaluated using the classical Neyman-Pearson theory, which is treated in introductory statistics textbooks (e.g., Glass & Hopkins, 1984; Hays, 1994). In most cases, a statistical test such as a t test or an analysis of variance is used to examine the likelihood that the means of the experimental and control groups are derived from a single-parent population and can be considered identical. The likelihood of this event is evaluated by some statistic (such as an F test in the analysis of variance). If the differences between the groups are sufficiently large so that this likelihood is less than an arbitrarily defined value, usually .05 or .01, it is concluded that the experimental and control groups are not sampled from the same parent population and that the independent variable has produced an effect on the dependent variable.

Similarity of the experimental and control groups in all characteristics other than the independent variable is achieved by the application of specific rules to assign subjects to the groups. In a matching procedure, the experimental and control groups are equated on presumably relevant background characteristics. For instance, the groups could have the same proportion of men and women if gender is assumed to influence the dependent variable. In random assignment, subjects are allocated at random to the experimental and control groups. The random allocation makes it unlikely that the two groups will be different in characteristics that are relevant for the dependent variable. Because the experimental and control groups can be taken not to differ on these characteristics, we usually feel quite confident about concluding that statistically significant differences between the two groups can be attributed to the independent variable.

Quasi-experiments are studies in which previously existing, intact groups are compared (Cook & Campbell, 1979). Cross-cultural studies fall into this category. The most important difference between treatments in the experimental tradition and in cross-cultural research is the control over the independent variables. When individuals from different cultures are studied, culture can be seen as an independent variable. However, whereas in true experimental designs the independent variable is fully manipulated by the researcher, culture is a variable that is beyond experimental control. In true experiments, subjects are assigned randomly to conditions; however, subjects cannot be assigned randomly to culture as a treatment in the same way as subjects are allocated to a group that will or will not receive a drug.

The implications of this lack of control are serious. For instance, the observation of significant cultural differences between first and fifth graders in Japan and the United States in tests on mathematics, reading, and cognitive abilities is interesting (Stevenson et al., 1986), but these findings alone cannot reveal the reasons for such differences. Why did the Japanese children show superior performance? A large number of differences between Japanese and American children can be put forward to explain these differences, ranging from genetic (e.g., Lynn, 1994) to cultural explanations such as parental influence (Sigel, 1988) and the time spent in school on reading and mathematics (Stigler, Lee, & Stevenson, 1987; Stigler & Perry, 1988). Observed cross-cultural differences on a focal variable can often be interpreted in numerous ways, and additional evidence is needed to evaluate the accuracy of different interpretations of these differences. Methodological considerations in carrying out cross-cultural research often center on the enhancement of the interpretability of observed cultural differences and on the reduction of the number of alternative explanations for these differences.

In true experiments, the differences between experimental and control groups in the dependent variable are attributed to the independent variable. The same reasoning can be applied to quasi-experiments; culture is then the independent variable. Differences between cultural groups can be attributed to culture. Culture is too global a concept to be meaningful as an explanatory variable, however, and should be replaced by its constituents (Kohn, 1987; Lonner & Adamopoulos, 1997; Poortinga & Malpass, 1986; Poortinga, van de Vijver, Joe, & Van de Koppel, 1987; van de Vijver & Leung, 1997; Whiting, 1976). These constituents are called context variables (e.g., Poortinga & van de Vijver, 1987) or cultural dimensions when they refer to culture-level phenomena. From a methodological perspective they are broadly defined as variables used to validate a particular interpretation of cross-cultural differences. Context variables can be person-related (such as age, gender, or psychological characteristics) or culture-related (such as gross national product, educational systems, and health care institutions).

The unpackaging of culture can be carried out in a verifying or falsifying way. Suppose that a reading achievement test is administered to pupils in Finland and Brazil, and that the researcher anticipates higher scores for the Finnish students. It is hypothesized that the number of hours spent on reading, rather than motivational factors, can explain the observed differences. A measurement of the number of hours of reading in the curriculum is aimed at verifying the interpretation; a positive relationship between reading achievement scores and number of hours spent on reading will provide evidence in support of the hypothesis. The absence of a relationship between motivational factors and reading achievement would falsify the role of motivation as an alternative explanation. The two different ways to decompose culture parallel the distinction between convergent and discriminant validity (Campbell & Fiske, 1959).

The process of unpackaging culture will usually consist of three steps. The first is substantive; it refers to the choice of appropriate context variables to verify or falsify a particular interpretation of cultural differences. The second aspect involves the design of the study: How will the context variables be measured? Finally, statistical techniques are required to evaluate the (lack of) success of the context variables explaining cross-cultural score differences; these techniques will be described in the fourth chapter (particularly in the section titled External Validation)

Bias as the Major Threat in Cross-Cultural Studies

The second issue is concerned with the control of bias. Probably more than any other field of psychology, cross-cultural studies are susceptible to measurement artifacts. All stages of a study have their own sources of bias. Three stages are of particular relevance in the present book: (a) the conceptualization of theoretical constructs relevant to the study and the formulation of research questions or hypotheses, (b) the design of the study, and (c) the data analysis. The choice of the theoretical constructs to be examined is usually one of the earliest decisions of a project and is already susceptible to the influence of bias (Berry, Poortinga, Segall, & Dasen, 1992). The constructs that are chosen may not be similarly defined in all cultural groups. Being a good son or daughter, for example, has somewhat different connotations and involves somewhat different behaviors in a Chinese and an American context (Ho, 1996).

The choice and administration of instruments can also introduce bias. Items can be inadequate. In an inventory of daily activities of elderly people, the item *Do you often visit your children?* may be appropriate in some countries but will be inappropriate in countries in which parents and children live in the same place or where children are expected to visit their parents. The inadequacy could also apply to the whole instrument. Suppose that Raven's matrices, a cognitive test, is administered to both literate and illiterate subjects. Differences in stimulus familiarity may be so large that overall differences in mean scores between these two groups mainly merely reflect this differential familiarity. Finally, the data analysis may introduce bias, called statistical conclusion invalidity by Cook and Campbell (1979). For instance, it is common to find that all items of an instrument are assumed to be equivalent across cultures without any statistical checks to support this claim.

We encourage the scrutiny of bias in all stages of a cross-cultural project. Unambiguous, interpretable cultural differences are the result of scrupulous theorizing, design, data collection, and analysis. As usual, the validity of the results is as good as the weakest link in this chain of activities. Insufficient control for alternative interpretations can substantially reduce the interpretability of the results of a study.

Plan of the Book

It is the task of the cross-cultural researcher both to explore and to explain (interpret) cross-cultural differences. These activities are inextricably linked. Explorations of cross-cultural differences have to be followed by explanations of these differences. Are the differences between Groups A and B in introversion due to measurement artifacts or to valid cross-cultural differences in introversion? In our view, the interpretation of cross-cultural differences is essential in a cross-cultural enterprise. A major part of the book is devoted to a discussion of factors threatening the interpretability of cross-cultural findings and how these threats can be reduced or even eliminated.

The second chapter presents our theoretical framework for cross-cultural comparison. Two essential concepts in these comparisons will be introduced, namely, equivalence and bias. The conditions under which valid cross-cultural comparisons can be made and the threats to valid cross-cultural comparisons will be discussed. A taxonomy of cross-cultural studies will be presented that provides an organizing framework for the discussion of various cross-cultural designs and data-analytic techniques in the subsequent chapters. The taxonomy makes a distinction among four types of studies, based on dichotomizing two dimensions. The first refers to the primary focus of a study that can be either exploratory or hypothesis testing; the second involves the presence or absence of context variables.

The third chapter describes the method and design of cross-cultural studies. The question of how a research design can be optimized to enhance the interpretability of cross-cultural differences is discussed in the first section. Choices to be made in the sampling of both cultures and subjects are described. Practical problems in the cross-cultural administration of research instruments are then discussed. The last section of the chapter deals with validity enhancement in two important areas of cross-cultural research: multilingual studies and assessment.

The fourth chapter describes the statistical analysis of cross-cultural data sets. In the introductory section a distinction is made between preliminary analyses aimed at the detection of anomalies in the measurement instruments used (discussed in the second section) and main analyses that address research questions or hypotheses (discussed in the third section).

The fifth chapter gives a more general description of design and analysis issues central to each of the four types of cross-cultural studies described in the second chapter.

The sixth chapter integrates the major issues in cross-cultural studies that have been discussed in the previous chapters and presents practical guidelines for conducting cross-cultural research. Finally, a future outlook is described.

2

Theoretical Background

Two closely related concepts play an essential role in cross-cultural comparisons, namely, equivalence and bias (Poortinga, 1989). From a theoretical point of view, the two concepts are the opposite of each other; scores are equivalent when they are unbiased. Nonetheless, the two concepts will be treated separately here because historically they have become associated with different aspects of cross-cultural comparisons. Equivalence is more often associated with the measurement level at which scores obtained in different cultural groups can be compared, whereas bias indicates the presence of factors that challenge the validity of cross-cultural comparisons.

An overview of biasing factors will be presented in the next section, followed by a description of the relationship between the biasing factors and the levels of equivalence distinguished. The last section will complete the theoretical background by providing a taxonomy of cross-cultural studies.

Equivalence

Levels of Equivalence

When an instrument measures different constructs in two cultures (i.e., when "apples and oranges are compared"), no comparison can be made. There is no link between scores obtained in one cultural group and scores obtained in other groups. We call this *construct inequivalence*. It can result from measurement problems. Constructs such as middle class or depression may have different meanings across cultures.

The same construct is measured in the case of *construct equivalence* (also labeled *structural equivalence*) even though not necessarily operationalized in the same way across cultures (van de Vijver & Leung, 1997). Suppose we are interested in the concept of shame. We ask local informants in two cultures to describe shame-inducing situations. These situations may turn out to show little overlap across cultures. Based on these situations, the instruments developed to measure shame will contain almost no identical stimuli. The instrument could well measure shame in each cultural group, but obviously the scores cannot be compared across cultures. The nomological networks of the instruments in the two cultures should be investigated to demonstrate construct equivalence (Cronbach & Meehl, 1955).

The next (and higher) level of equivalence is known as *measurement unit equivalence*. A simple example is the measurement of temperature using Kelvin and Celsius scales. The measurement unit is identical in both groups but the origins of the scales are not; by subtracting 273 from the temperatures in Celsius, these will be converted into degrees Kelvin. Unfortunately, we hardly ever know the offset of scales in cross-cultural research. Suppose that an intelligence test developed in Sweden has been administered in Sweden and a translation of it in Turkey. The test material may contain various implicit and explicit references to the Swedish culture. These references will put Turkish subjects at a disadvantage. As a consequence, the (supposedly) interval-level scores in each group do not constitute comparability at ratio level.

The last (and highest) level of equivalence has been called *scalar equivalence* or *full score comparability*. This level of equivalence can be achieved when the measurement instrument is on the same ratio scale in each cultural group. Examples are the measurement of body length (in centimeters or inches) and weight (in kilograms or pounds). Scalar equivalence will also be achieved when scores on an instrument have the same interval scale across cultural groups. This refers to a useful characteristic of interval scales: Differences on an interval scale are measured at ratio level. For example, when temperatures are measured using a Celsius scale (which is of interval level), differences in temperature are measured at ratio level.

The Need to Establish Equivalence

Establishing the Level of Comparability

There seems to be a widely held view that equivalence is an intrinsic property of an instrument: Some instruments are taken to yield fully equivalent scores in each and every cross-cultural comparison. In our view, it may be more productive to adopt a functional view and to consider equivalence as a property of a specific cross-cultural comparison. Equivalence is a function of characteristics of an instrument and of the cultural groups involved. Suppose that the WISC-R, an intelligence test for children, is administered to first graders in Senegal, Belgium, and Florida. To some degree, the presence of bias will depend on the instrument. Instruments that require knowledge obtained in schools may show more bias than, say, a test of memory span. Bias will also depend on the cultural distance between the groups. Cross-cultural comparisons of youngsters from Belgium and Florida are less likely to be biased than comparisons involving the Senegalese group because formal education, an important aspect in performance on mental tests, will differ between Senegal and the other places.

Claims about the level of equivalence, particularly scalar equivalence, can be controversial. Scalar equivalence is sometimes claimed when construct equivalence has been established. More specifically, when an exploratory factor analysis of a personality questionnaire shows essentially similar loadings in various cultural groups, it is often argued that scores on the instrument show scalar equivalence. This claim can be challenged along two lines. First, the measurement units need not be the same across cultural groups. When all scores are doubled in one group, the cross-cultural differences will be affected, but factor loadings remain unaffected. Moreover, scores may show measurement unit equivalence instead of scalar equivalence. Bias that affects all stimuli of an instrument in more or less the same way cannot be detected by factor analysis. Both arguments against the use of factor analysis to establish scalar equivalence derive from the fact that such an analysis takes correlations as input. Linear transformations (of the form $Y = aX + b$ with $a > 0$) have an impact on raw scores (and, hence, on the observed cross-cultural differences) but not on correlations. Statistical techniques that are insensitive to such linear transformations can never be used to substantiate scalar equivalence.

The cross-cultural application of intelligence tests has also led to sharp debates about the equivalence level. Do intelligence tests yield scalar (ratio-level) or measurement unit (interval-level) equivalence? For instance, Jensen (1980) has argued that given that a proper test is used, such as Raven's Progressive Matrices (Raven, 1938), cross-cultural differences in intellectual functioning can be adequately assessed. In contrast, Mercer (1984) maintains that a critical inspection of the contents of common intelligence tests and their psychometric properties can only suggest the presence of bias. Cross-cultural differences as measured by common intelligence tests can at best reach measurement-unit equivalence in her reasoning. We find that such debates are often sterile from a theoretical point of view and quickly lead to a deadlock, as the IQ debate illustrates. Without additional evidence to substantiate a particular interpretation of cross-cultural differences, such stalemates are hard to resolve. Our position is more pragmatic: We acknowledge that the level of equivalence is usually unknown in empirical studies. Therefore, equivalence cannot be assumed but should be established and reported in each study. In Chapter 4, we will describe various statistical procedures to examine equivalence.

Bias: Definitions, Sources, and Detection

Bias is a generic term for all nuisance factors threatening the validity of cross-cultural comparisons. Poor item translations, inappropriate item content, and lack of standardization in administration procedures are just a few examples. We will present three types of bias in the present section: construct, method, and item bias. Sources of each of these will be described. Procedures to detect and overcome these types of bias are so varied that they cannot be adequately discussed in a single chapter. Procedures for overcoming construct bias are described in the next section; similar procedures for method bias are discussed in Chapter 3

TABLE 2.1 Overview of Types of Bias and Their Most Common Causes (after van de Vijver & Poortinga, 1997, p. 26)

Type of Bias	Source
Construct	• incomplete overlap of definitions of the construct across cultures • differential appropriateness of (sub)test content (e.g., skills do not belong to the repertoire of one of the cultural groups) • poor sampling of all relevant behaviors (e.g., short instruments) • incomplete coverage of the construct (e.g., not all relevant domains are sampled)
Method	• differential social desirability • differential response styles such as extremity scoring and acquiescence • differential stimulus familiarity • lack of comparability of samples (e.g., differences in educational background, age, or gender composition) • differences in physical conditions of administration • differential familiarity with response procedures • tester/interviewer effects • communication problems between respondent and tester/interviewer in either cultural group
Item	• poor item translation • inadequate item formulation (e.g., complex wording) • item(s) may invoke additional traits or abilities • incidental differences in appropriateness of the item content (e.g., topic of item of educational test not in curriculum in one cultural group)

SOURCE: Used by permission from Hogrefe & Huber Publishers, Seattle, Toronto, Bern, Göttingen.

under Validity Enhancement, and for item bias in Chapter 4 under Item Bias Analysis.

Construct Bias

The first type of bias is called *construct bias*. It will occur when the construct measured is not identical across cultural groups (see Table 2.1). Studies in Western (Sternberg, 1985; Sternberg, Conway, Ketron, & Bernstein, 1981) as well as non-Western (Serpell, 1993; Super, 1983) countries have shown that everyday conceptions of intelligence are broader than the domain covered by most Western intelligence tests. In addition to reasoning components, everyday conceptions of intelligence encompass social aspects. Obedience, the ability to deal with complex social situations, and various other interpersonal skills are part of everyday conceptions, particularly in non-Western contexts. Because of the absence of the social component in common instruments, these are probably more adequately called tests of academic or scholastic intelligence.

Construct bias can also be induced by a lack of overlap in behaviors associated with the construct in the cultures studied. Ho (1996) has studied the concept of filial piety, being a good son or daughter. He found that the behaviors associated with being a good son or daughter, such as taking care of one's parents, conforming to their requests, and treating them well, are much broader in China than in most Western countries. Similarly, Kuo and Marsella (1977), studying Machiavellianism in China and the United States, argued that differences in "behavioral referents, correlates, and functional implications" (p. 165) question the equivalence of the construct in the two countries. A final example comes from ethnopsychiatry in which various culture-bound syndromes are studied, such as *latah,* an exaggerated startle response in some Southeast Asian groups, and *koro,* a fear among Chinese males that their penis will withdraw into their abdominal cavity (see Guthrie & Lonner, 1986).

A poor sampling of a domain in the instrument can give rise to construct bias. Broad constructs are often represented by a small number of items in a questionnaire or test. Embretson (1983) has coined the term *construct underrepresentation* to refer to this insufficient sampling of a behavioral domain. For instance, if most items of a measure of coping depict interpersonal situations, the instrument will yield a poor insight into intrapersonal coping mechanisms and will not generalize to instruments with a broader or differently focused item pool.

Leung and Zhang (1996) have pointed to another source of construct bias: Many studies have been exported from the West to non-Western countries, and some of the issues examined in these studies are of little relevance to non-Western cultures. In a similar vein, Moghaddam (1990) has argued that educational psychology in the West is geared toward a literate population, and this orientation is inadequate for some countries because a significant portion of their population is illiterate. The Chinese Culture Connection (1987) raised an even more fundamental question about the importation of Western psychological knowledge into non-Western countries. It is easily conceivable that results obtained in Western countries are shaped by the cultural background of the researchers, and that different results are obtained if the cultural vantage point of non-Western countries is taken.

In some cases the presence of construct bias can be studied using factor analysis or some other technique aimed at detecting the structure underlying an instrument. Cross-cultural differences in factor-analytic solutions (e.g., in factor structures) point to construct bias. However, the presence of construct bias cannot always be decided upon from a simple administration of the instrument. If an instrument measuring filial piety is administered in both a Chinese and an American context, a comparison of averages or factor structures will not show the (in)adequacy of the instrument. A study of construct bias will require the collection of additional data to investigate the applicability of the construct and instrument. If there is suspicion that the constructs will not be identical across cultures or will entail dissimilar behaviors, a local survey can be carried out asking informants to describe the construct and its characteristic behaviors (see Serpell, 1993; Super, 1983).

Two approaches may be adopted to design a culturally balanced study in which no single culture would dominate the research questions explored and the design of the study. First, a *decentered* approach can be adopted, in which a culturally diverse perspective is taken in the conceptualization and design of a study (Werner & Campbell, 1970). As an example, Schwartz (1992), testing his pan-cultural model of value structure, encouraged researchers from different cultures to add culture-specific value items to his pan-cultural set. Smith and Peterson (1988) have taken into account the influence of culture in their formulation of a theory of leadership behavior. They argued that the context in which leadership behavior occurs should be taken into account in understanding the meaning of such behavior. The role of culture in shaping the interpretation of the meaning of leadership behavior constitutes a central part of their theory. Data from cross-cultural research are used to support their approach (Peterson et al., 1995).

The second approach is the *convergence* approach. Suppose that a phenomenon is studied in a set of cultures. A researcher from each culture will design his or her own instrument, each of which will be administered in all cultures (Campbell, 1986). Similarity of findings across instruments (e.g., the same patterning of cross-cultural differences) provides strong evidence for the validity of the observed cross-cultural differences, whereas discrepancies could point to interesting sources of bias.

A related approach is to design a study that is as culturally distant as possible from existing studies and to see if the obtained results coincide with existing results. If they coincide, it can be concluded that the cultural origin of earlier studies did not bias the results. If different results are obtained, however, the impact of the cultural origin has to be further investigated. The best examples to illustrate this approach are provided by Bond and his colleagues. The Chinese Culture Connection (1987) designed a value survey based entirely on Chinese values and administered it in 22 countries. It was found that three factors were similar to those identified by Hofstede (1980), whose results were based on a Western instrument. A new factor was also identified, named Confucian work dynamism, which correlated highly with economic growth. In the realm of person perception, Yang and Bond (1990) administered a set of emic Chinese descriptors together with a set of imported American descriptors to a group of Taiwanese subjects. Of the five Chinese factors identified, only four corresponded to American factors.

Both the decentered and the convergence approaches are useful for establishing theories that are likely to be universal. The decentered approach is easier to follow as it only requires supplementing and broadening concepts developed in the West. Despite its simplicity, this procedure is only occasionally followed in the literature. Many cross-cultural studies are still designed with the aim of testing whether a certain theory, typically developed in the West, will work in a different cultural setting. This "let's see if it will work there" orientation tends to reduce the motivation of researchers to gain an in-depth understanding of the cultures that they study. Although it is now standard practice to invite collaborators from cultures that one wants to study, their role is often to gather data rather than to enrich the theoretical basis and the design of the study. As a result, the usefulness of cultural considerations for improving the breadth and depth of theories is attenuated. In our opinion, all cross-cultural studies should be culturally decentered in the design phase, and we see this procedure as crucial to the use of cross-cultural work as a vehicle for major theoretical breakthroughs.

The convergence approach is usually difficult to carry out as it involves the development of indigenous research materials and requires a substantial amount of resources and time. For instance, developing a personality inventory for the Chinese people, the Chinese Personality Assessment Inventory, took 4 years of research work by a team of about 10 researchers and research assistants, several pilot studies involving more than 2,000 subjects from different demographic groups, and a main study involving more than 2,000 subjects (Cheung et al., 1996). The inherent practical difficulty of the convergence approach probably explains why it is rarely followed. Nevertheless, we believe that this is an indispensable way to correct the strong reliance on the Western cultural perspective in the development of psychology as a universal science.

Method Bias

Even if a construct is well represented in an instrument, there is no guarantee that there will be no bias in the scores. Bias could arise from particular characteristics of the instrument or its administration. This will be called *method bias*, because such bias arises from aspects described in the Method section of research reports. Table 2.1 gives an overview of common sources of method bias.

Differential response styles such as acquiescence and extremity ratings can constitute method bias. A demonstration can be found in the work of Hui and Triandis (1989). These authors found that Hispanics tended to choose extremes on a 5-point rating scale more often than did White Americans, while no significant cross-cultural differences were found for 10-point scales. Ross and Mirowsky (1984) reported more acquiescence and socially desirable responses among Mexicans than among Anglo-Americans in a mental health survey.

A common source of method bias in mental testing is differential familiarity with the stimuli used. Back in the 1940s, Cattell attempted to resolve this problem by using simple geometric stimuli; he reasoned that tests that use very simple stimuli are free from cultural influences. This led to the development of "culture-free tests" (Cattell, 1940). When it was realized that this assumption was untenable, "culture-fair tests" were developed (Cattell & Cattell, 1963). Stimuli in these tests were designed in such a way that they would not be differentially affected by cultural background. Not surprisingly, the existence of culture-free and culture-fair tests has been seriously criticized (e.g., Faucheux, 1976; Frijda & Jahoda, 1966). When cognitive tests are administered to cultural groups with widely different educational backgrounds, differences in stimulus familiarity are almost impossible to overcome, especially when Western tests are used.

Response procedures can also show differential familiarity across cultures. Good illustrations can be found in Serpell's work. He asked

Zambian and British children to reproduce a pattern using paper and pencil, plasticine, configurations of hand positions, and iron wire (making models with iron wire is a popular pastime among Zambian boys) (Serpell, 1979). The British scored significantly higher when they used the paper-and-pencil procedure, whereas the Zambians scored higher when iron wires were used; no significant differences were found for the other media. Deregowksi and Serpell (1971) asked Scottish and Zambian children to sort miniature models of animals and motor vehicles and in another condition to sort photographs of these models. No cross-cultural differences were found for the actual models, whereas the Scottish children obtained higher scores than the Zambian children when photographs were sorted.

Differences in physical conditions during administration can also lead to method bias. Examples are noise in the environment or the presence of other people. When speeded tests are administered or when reaction times are measured in computerized testing, equality of testing conditions (e.g., the lighting conditions, the response device, and the distance between the subject and the screen) can be critical. An administration protocol clearly describing the conditions of administration will alleviate many of these problems.

A final source of method bias can be communication problems between the examiner/interviewer and the examinee/interviewee. These could arise from differential interviewing skills and language problems, because it is not uncommon in cross-cultural studies to find that the testing or interview language is the second or third language of interviewers, respondents, or even both. Communication problems could also arise from the use of locally inappropriate modes of address or other violations of local norms.

Method bias usually affects scores at the level of the whole instrument. In statistical terms, method bias will be found in the data as a significant effect for cultural group in a t test or a significant main effect of cultural group in an analysis of variance (assuming that the method bias is sufficiently large to reach statistical significance). We do not adhere to the frequently adopted practice of treating such significant effects (or impact as it is often called in the Anglo-Saxon literature, e.g., Holland & Wainer, 1993) invariably as indicators of valid differences. In our view, significant cross-cultural differences can be a mixture of valid cross-cultural differences and bias effects, in particular method bias.

Several procedures can be envisaged to study the influence of administration problems. The first, mainly suitable for cognitive tests, entails the repeated administration of the same instrument in various cultural groups and the examination of score changes, usually score increments, upon retesting. If subjects with similar scores on the pretest show differential gain patterns, strong evidence for method bias has been obtained. Gain patterns on cognitive tests that are larger in non-Western groups than in Western groups have been reported (e.g., Kendall, Verster, & Von Mollendorf, 1988; van de Vijver, Daal, & Van Zonneveld, 1986). Nkaya, Huteau, and Bonnet (1994) administered Raven's Standard Matrices three times to sixth graders in France and the Congo. When no time limit was applied, there was a moderate improvement from the first to the second and no progress from the second to the third administration in both groups. Under timed conditions, however, both groups progressed rapidly from the first to the second, but only the Congolese pupils progressed from the second to the third session. Such a finding retrospectively casts doubt on the validity of the first administration. Ombrédane, Robaye, and Plumail (1956) have shown that repeated test administrations can also affect the relationship with external measures. The predictive validity of the Raven's test score was found to increase after repeated administration in a group of illiterate Congolese mine workers.

A second way to assess method bias is the systematic variation of stimuli across cultures. Through systematic variation of stimulus contents or response modes, insight is gained into the consistency of the various responses. Such a variation is particularly useful for cross-cultural research because each type of stimulus content or response mode may have its own limitations (Triandis, 1992). A low consistency of responses points to method bias. Examples of such systematic variations are monotrait-multimethod designs (e.g., Marsh & Byrne, 1993) and triangulation (e.g., Lipson & Meleis, 1989; see also discussion in Chapter 3, Validity Enhancement in Assessment).

Item Bias

The third kind of bias, *item bias*, refers to measurement artifacts at item level. In the Anglo-Saxon literature the term has been largely replaced by *differential item functioning*, or its acronym, *dif*. We do not follow this habit, because we want to emphasize in our choice of terminology that item bias, like construct and method bias, is a measurement problem that, if not properly attended to, jeopardizes the validity of cross-cultural comparisons.

Item bias can be produced by various sources such as incidental differences in appropriateness of the item content (e.g., some items of an educational test are not in the curriculum in one cultural group), inadequate item formulation (e.g., complex wording), and inadequate translation. An example can be found in the European Value Survey (Halman, May 1996, personal communication). This scale of value orientations contained an item about loyalty. The Spanish-language version yielded cross-cultural differences that were highly different from those on other items. Upon closer examination it appeared that, unlike in other languages, the Spanish word that was used for *loyalty* has the connotation of sexual faithfulness.

Another source of item bias is incidental inappropriateness of item content. Amirkhan's coping questionnaire has the item *Watched more television than usual* as one of the items measuring avoidance, one of the three coping strategies assessed. When the questionnaire was applied to groups of Sahel dwellers without electricity in their homes, the item had to be removed (Van Haaften & van de Vijver, 1996). In Chapter 4, Item Bias Analysis, techniques will be discussed to identify biased items.

Implications of Bias for Equivalence

The equivalence levels discussed above in Levels of Equivalence (construct, measurement unit, and scalar) and the taxonomy of bias above in Bias: Definitions, Sources, and Detection (construct, method, item) are related to each other. In general, bias will lower the level of equivalence. Construct bias will tend to preclude any direct score comparison (see Table 2.2). In the case of method and item bias, we introduce a distinction between uniform and nonuniform bias (see also Chapter 4, Item Bias Analysis). *Uniform bias* refers to influences of bias on scores that are more or less the same for all score levels. As an example, suppose that we measure body weight but that the measure in one

TABLE 2.2 Is Level of Equivalence Affected by Bias?

		Level of Equivalence	
Type of Bias	*Construct*	*Measurement Unit*[a]	*Scalar*[a, b]
Construct bias	no	no	no
Method bias: uniform	yes	yes	no
nonuniform	yes	no	no
Item bias: uniform	yes	yes	no
nonuniform	yes	no	no

a. The same measurement unit is assumed in each cultural group.
b. The same origin is assumed in each cultural group.

group consistently shows 1 kilogram too much. *Nonuniform* bias refers to influences that are not identical for all score levels. Suppose that our measurement for measuring weight is accurate in one group but that in the other group 1 kg on the scale is actually 1.1 kg. The difference in measured weights of two objects with a real weight of 20 kg will be 2 kg, but when the real weight is 100 kg, the difference will be 10 kg. Cross-cultural comparisons involving higher weights will be more distorted.

Both method and item bias can give rise to uniform and nonuniform bias. This bias is harmless for construct equivalence, because numeric score comparisons across cultures are not permitted anyway. Uniform bias will not threaten measurement unit equivalence; even unbiased scores at this level of equivalence could not be directly compared across cultures (due to a different origin in each cultural group), and adding a constant to all scores in a single group does not affect this type of equivalence. The introduction of uniform bias to scores that show scalar equivalence will lead to the loss of this type of equivalence. When a constant is added to all scores in one group, the differences in scores between groups no longer have a natural origin; therefore, uniform bias will lead here to measurement unit equivalence. Nonuniform bias will destroy equivalence to a considerable extent because the measurement units in the two groups are no longer the same. When several items show this kind of bias, cross-cultural score comparisons are likely to produce incorrect results.

TABLE 2.3   Four Common Types of Cross-Cultural Studies

Consideration of Contextual Factors	Orientation More on	
	Hypothesis Testing	*Exploration*
No	Generalizability	Psychological differences
Yes	Theory-driven	External validation

SOURCE: van de Vijver & Leung, 1997. Used by permission from Allyn & Bacon.

A Taxonomy of Cross-Cultural Studies

Four Common Types of Comparative Studies

Cultural studies vary on two dimensions. The first dimension makes a distinction between exploratory and hypothesis-driven studies. In exploratory studies, researchers do not have firm ideas about the cross-cultural similarities and differences to be expected. Such occasions are likely to arise when researchers venture into cultures that are unknown to them. Alternatively, there may be insufficient previous research for generating specific hypotheses.

The second dimension addresses the use of context variables to explain cultural similarities and/or observed differences. Such context variables may be demographic in nature, such as educational level, age, and marital status. Psychological variables may also be included, such as values, personality traits, attitudes, beliefs, and cognitive styles. In some studies no context variables are included, and the goal of the study is simply to document cultural similarities and differences. In other studies, context variables are included for illuminating the likely causes of cultural similarities and differences. To simplify the discussion, the two dimensions are dichotomized. Four types of cross-cultural studies can be identified by crossing these two dimensions. See Table 2.3 for a schematic presentation of these four types of studies.

The first two types emphasize hypothesis testing. *Generalizability studies* attempt to establish the generalizability of research findings obtained in one group, typically a Western group, to other Western or non-Western groups. In general, these studies make little or no reference to cultural elements other than the target variables on which cultures are compared.

In the second type, called *theory-driven studies*, specific aspects of a culture such as its ecology, way of raising children, or particular cultural habits are part of the theoretical framework upon which the design of a study is based. Cultural variation on these specific aspects is deliberately sought as a way to validate a theoretical model. Specific a priori predictions are tested in these studies. This can only be done by sampling various cultures that differ on target dimensions. Contextual elements are crucial in these studies.

Hypothesis testing is de-emphasized in the following two types of cross-cultural research. The first type, *psychological differences studies*, is most common in the cross-cultural literature. A measurement instrument is applied in at least two cultures, and the researcher is interested in whether or not there are any cross-cultural differences in the means, standard deviations, reliability coefficients, nomological networks, or structures underlying the instrument. The researcher wants to explore cross-cultural differences, but no theory is available for predicting the nature of the cross-cultural differences that may be found. Context variables are typically not included in the design, and post hoc explanations are often invoked to interpret the observed cross-cultural differences.

The last type of cross-cultural research, *external validation studies*, attempts to explore the meaning and causes of cross-cultural differences with the aid of context variables. Specific a priori hypotheses are absent, and usually a large set of context variables are included in an exploratory manner. Regression analysis is the most frequently applied technique for assessing the ability of context variables to explain cross-cultural variations in the dependent variable. This procedure does not usually address issues of structural or scalar equivalence but seeks to identify variables that help to interpret observed cross-cultural differences.

Level and Structure Orientation in the Four Types of Cross-Cultural Studies

Two major orientations can be distinguished in cross-cultural studies: *structure-oriented* and *level-oriented*. Structure-oriented studies focus on relationships among variables and attempt to identify similarities and differences in these relationships across cultures. For example, is the structure of values similar across cultures? Are the nomological

networks of conformity different across cultures? Level-oriented studies, on the other hand, focus on differences in magnitude of variables
across cultures. For example, do members of Culture A show a higher
level of external locus of control than members of Culture B?

Each of the four types of cross-cultural studies described above can
adopt either a structure or a level orientation (though the frequency of
applications of both orientations is not equal for the four types).

Generalizability Studies

An example of a structure-oriented generalizability study is provided by Schwartz's (1992) work on the structure of values. Another example is the cross-cultural research on the universality of the five-factor
model of personality (e.g., Church & Katigbak, 1989; De Raad, 1994;
McCrae & Costa, 1985; McCrae, Zonderman, Costa, Bond, & Paunonen,
1996). The goal of this line of work is to establish the universality of the
big-five structure of personality (neuroticism, extroversion, openness
to experience, agreeableness, and conscientiousness). Another example
is provided by the work on the "big-seven" model of natural language
trait descriptors (Almagor, Tellegen, & Waller, 1995). This line of work
attempts to establish the universality of seven factors in natural language trait descriptors. Buss (1989) examined the cross-cultural stability
of differences of mate preferences of men and women in various countries (see Hatfield & Sprecher, 1995). A study of the choice of conflict
resolution procedures (Leung, 1987) is an example of a cross-cultural
study of a causal relationship. In this study, the relative importance of
several determinants of preference for different conflict resolution procedures was evaluated in Hong Kong and in the United States.

A level-oriented generalizability study is provided by Bochner
(1994). Trafimow, Triandis, and Goto (1991) found that American subjects showed a higher level of idiocentric cognitions in their self-concept
than did Chinese subjects. That is, American subjects were more likely
to describe themselves with personal qualities, attitudes, or behaviors
that do not relate to others. On the other hand, Chinese subjects showed
a higher level of group cognitions in their self-concept than did American subjects. Chinese subjects were more likely to describe themselves
as members of certain groups. Bochner (1994) examined the generalizability of these findings to cultures other than the United States and
China. He used Malaysians to represent collectivists and Australians

and British to represent individualists. The results obtained by Trafimow et al. (1991) were replicated with this new set of cultural groups. This study is level-oriented because the focus is on cultural differences in the frequency of difference types of self-cognitions reported. The study belongs to the generalizability category because no context variables were used. Another example is provided by Amir and Sharon (1987), who replicated a number of well-known Western social psychological studies with Israeli subjects. The authors were interested in the generalizability of findings from experimental social psychology obtained among Western subjects to an Israeli context. An experiment was taken to be generalizable if the same main effects and interactions were significant in the Israeli replication. The authors found that significant main effects could often be replicated but that interaction effects did not generalize well and, when they were significant, the direction of the effects was often different from the original findings.

Theory-Driven Studies

A structure-oriented example of a theory-driven study is provided by the work of Sidanius, Pratto, and Rabinowitz (1994). Basing their work on social dominance theory, the authors proposed that for members of high-status ethnic groups, social dominance orientation (i.e., the desire to establish hierarchical social relationships among social groups) should be positively related to group salience and differential group closeness. *Group salience* refers to the experienced salience of one's ethnic group membership, and *differential group closeness* refers to the emotional closeness of one's ethnic group to other ethnic groups. The stronger the social dominance orientation, the more salient is one's ethnic identity and the closer one feels toward one's ethnic group. For members of low-status groups, however, the relationship between social dominance orientation and group salience and differential group closeness should be weaker. This prediction was tested in the United States with a group of Whites, the high-status ethnic group, and a group of Blacks and Hispanics, the low-status groups. Using structural equation modeling, Sidanius et al. confirmed their hypothesis. Results showed that for White subjects, social dominance orientation was positively related to group salience and differential group closeness, whereas for Black and Hispanic subjects, social dominance was negatively related to these variables.

An example of a level-oriented theory-driven study is provided by Berry's (1966, 1976) work on cognitive style. Basing his work on the ecocultural framework, Berry argued that visual discrimination, visual disembedding, and spatial orientation should be more important for survival for hunters and gatherers than for members of agricultural groups. Thus, hunters and gatherers should be more field independent, whereas members of agricultural groups should be more field dependent. *Field independence* is the tendency to use internal frames of reference such as bodily cues to orient oneself in space, whereas *field dependence* is the tendency to use external visual cues. Berry tested and confirmed the hypothesis that members of a hunting group were more field independent, whereas members of an agricultural group were more field dependent. The study involved a comparison of Canadian hunter-gatherers and African agriculturists. Interestingly, when the study was replicated in Central Africa with groups that were more related culturally, the pattern of findings was much more complex and only partially supported the original hypothesis (Berry et al., 1986). Another example can be found in Earley's (1989) work on social loafing (the phenomenon that people work less when they are in a group than when they have to do the same work alone). American subjects were found to show more social loafing than Chinese subjects. Measures for individualism and collectivism were also collected from all subjects. Introduction of these scores as covariates made the cross-cultural differences disappear.

Psychological Differences Studies

Psychological differences studies abound in the literature; many empirical papers in journals publishing cross-cultural studies, such as the *Journal of Cross-Cultural Psychology*, the *International Journal of Psychology*, and the *International Journal of Comparative Sociology*, fall into this category. An example of a *structure-oriented design* is provided by Russell and Sato (1995; see Chapter 4, Structure-Oriented Techniques). They studied the meaning and equivalence of emotion words among English-speaking, Japanese-speaking, and Cantonese-speaking individuals. A set of 14 photographs of faces was shown to the subjects, and they were asked to judge to what extent the face shown in the picture was an expression of each of 14 emotion words. For any two language groups, a correlation index for an emotion word can be calculated based on the ratings of these groups on the 14 photographs. The higher the correlation, the more similar is the meaning of the emotion word across the two languages. Three comparison groups could be formed: English/Japanese, English/Cantonese, and Japanese/Cantonese, and these three groups could be compared on the correlations of the 14 emotion words. Results showed that the correlations were similar across the three comparison groups for 12 of the 14 emotion words. The study is structure-oriented because the key dependent variables are correlation coefficients; furthermore, the study belongs to the psychological differences category because no context variables were included and no hypotheses about cross-cultural differences were made.

Level-oriented studies in the psychological differences category are also popular in the literature. For instance, Guida and Ludlow (1989) examined cross-cultural differences in test anxiety between American and Chilean schoolchildren. The latter group was found to display higher levels of test anxiety. As is common for psychological differences studies, no attempt was made to evaluate causal antecedents for these differences in this study.

External Validation Studies

In the category of external validation, an example of a *structure-oriented design* is provided by Diener and Diener (1995). In a study of college students from 31 nations, Diener and Diener obtained correlations between overall life satisfaction and each of four variables: self-esteem, satisfaction with family, satisfaction with friends, and satisfaction with finances. For each nation, four correlations were available for further analysis. That is, nation was treated as the unit of analysis (see Chapter 4, External Validation, for a more detailed specification of this analysis). The correlations were transformed into normally distributed variables, and each of the four transformed correlations was correlated with the individualism-collectivism score of the 31 nations. It was predicted and found that the transformed correlation between self-esteem and overall life satisfaction correlated positively with individualism-collectivism. The correlation between self-esteem and overall life satisfaction was higher in individualistic cultures than in collectivist cultures. This aspect of the study falls in the structure-oriented, theory-driven category. Diener and Diener also explored whether the relationship between the size of the self-esteem/ overall life satisfaction correlation and individualism was qualified by the variability of self-esteem and life satisfaction within each nation. Variability of these two variables was operationalized as their standard deviation within each nation. When variability was controlled for, the relationship between the self-esteem/overall life satisfaction correlation and individualism remained unchanged. The effect of the status of the college that subjects attended was controlled for in a similar fashion, and the impact of individualism on the relationship between self-esteem and overall life satisfaction again remained unchanged. To sum up, the observed relationship between the self-esteem/overall life satisfaction correlation and individualism was due neither to variability in self-esteem and overall life satisfaction across nations, nor to status of the college that subjects attended. This aspect of the study falls in the external validation category because no hypotheses were made with regard to the effects of the status variable and the variability in self-esteem and overall satisfaction. Their inclusion in the study was purely for exploratory purposes.

An example of a *level-oriented study* in the external validation category can be found in the work of Bond (1991) on the relationship between values and health measures across countries. In this study, two value dimensions derived from the Chinese Value Survey, integration versus inwardness and reputation versus morality, were correlated with a host of measures related to health, including longevity measures, modes of death, health endangering behaviors, and indicators of social well-being. Social integration, which taps an essential component of individualism, is correlated with several causes of death. Reputation, which emphasizes material success, was correlated with two types of coronary heart diseases. As another example, Williams and Best (1982, 1990; Best & Williams, 1994) studied relationships between cross-national differences in sex stereotypes and demographic variables (such as GNP, educational level, and religious denomination). They found, among other things, that "national development may be accompanied by a reduction in the degree in which women and men are viewed as 'psychologically different' " (Williams & Best, 1990, p. 253). The observed differences in sex stereotypes and in masculinity/femininity were unrelated to Hofstede's masculinity variable, possibly due to the different conceptualizations and measures of these constructs.

3

Methods and Design

Selecting Cultures, Subjects, and Procedures

Sampling of Cultures

Three procedures for sampling cultures can be discerned. In *convenience sampling*, researchers select a culture simply because of considerations of convenience. These considerations can derive from various sources: Researchers may be from that culture, be acquainted with collaborators from that culture, or happen to have stayed there for a period of time. The choice of culture is not related to the theoretical questions raised and is often haphazard. Studies adopting this sampling scheme often fall into the category of psychological differences studies.

The second procedure is *systematic sampling*, in which cultures are selected in a systematic, theory-guided fashion. These studies usually fall into the categories of theory-driven or generalizability studies. Cultures are selected in this procedure because they represent different values on a theoretical continuum. The classic study by Berry (1976) discussed in Chapter 2, Level and Structure Orientation in the Four Types of Cross-Cultural Studies, provides an example. Another example of this approach is provided by Leung, Au, Fernandez-Dols, and Iwawaki (1992), who selected four cultures, namely, Spain, Japan, Canada, and The Netherlands. Japan and Spain are more collectivist, whereas Canada and The Netherlands are more individualistic (Hofstede, 1980). The comparison of these two pairs of countries will reveal the impact of individualism-collectivism. On the other hand, Spain and The Netherlands are more feminine, whereas Japan and Canada are more masculine (Hofstede, 1980). The comparison of Spain and The Netherlands with Japan and Canada will reveal the effects of cultural masculinity and femininity. An interesting feature of this study is that in both types of comparison, each group is composed of a Western and an Eastern culture. If differences are found between the two groups, the possibility that the differences are due to general East-West differences can be ruled out.

We believe that in the systematic approach, bicultural comparisons are adequate only if the results can be interpreted within a compelling theoretical framework. If a study is exploratory, or if the theoretical framework available is tentative, it is preferable to include three or more cultural groups. Campbell (1986) argued that the number of rival explanations can be greatly reduced when the number of cultures employed increases (assuming that the cultures can be ordered along a dimension that is relevant to the phenomenon studied).

To maximize the effectiveness of systematic sampling, effort should be made to select cultures that are far apart on the theoretical dimension on which they vary. This strategy will maximize the possibility of detecting cultural differences if they truly exist. However, highly dissimilar cultures are likely to be different in many other aspects as well, and numerous alternative interpretations have to be ruled out. As pointed out before, the use of several cultures will sidestep this problem. The general rule is simple: The larger the number of cultures studied, the more compelling is the conclusion that the observed cross-cultural score differences can be validly attributed to the theoretical dimensions of interest.

The third procedure is *random sampling*, which involves the sampling of a large number of cultures randomly. This strategy is preferable for generalizability studies, in which a universal structure or a pan-cultural theory is evaluated. Obviously, it is almost impossible to collect a truly random sample of cultures because of constraints of time and resources. When enough cultures are involved, a random sampling (of at least Western cultures) may eventually be approximated. For instance, Schwartz (1992, 1994) has sampled 36 cultures to evaluate the structure of human values, and his strategy is to include any cultural group in which he could find a collaborator. Buss (1989) followed a similar approach in sampling 37 cultures in his study of mate selection. Peterson et al. (1995) surveyed managers from more than 20 countries on event management issues. Smith, Dugan, and Trompenaars (1996) studied the values of employees in 43 countries.

These three sampling schemes serve different purposes. Systematic and random sampling of cultures are usually to be preferred. Convenience sampling is least costly, but is likely to lead to interpretation problems. If similarity is observed across the samples, it can be claimed that some evidence is obtained for the generality of the results. If no similarity is observed, however, it may be difficult to advance an adequate explanation of the results obtained. No pertinent data will be available to support the interpretation and only post hoc explanations can be offered.

The choice of cultures is often less obvious in exploratory studies, because no theoretical basis may be available for guiding a systematic sampling procedure. Random sampling is usually impractical. In this situation, we propose that researchers consider whether their primary objective is to look for differences or to look for universality. If the objective is to look for differences, it may be more informative to start with cultures that are more similar. For instance, Germans can be compared with Swedes because the two countries are similar in many aspects due to their geographical proximity and similarity in economic wealth. These similarities will greatly reduce the number of alternative explanations. Cross-cultural differences obtained in this context are more informative than differences obtained between a German town and a fishing village somewhere in China. The numerous differences between urban Germany and rural China caused by different levels of economic development make the interpretation of cross-cultural differences very difficult. On the other hand, if the primary objective is to look for universal patterns, it would be more informative to include cultures that are as different as possible. If similar findings can be obtained from urban Germans and rural fishermen in China, a strong claim for universality can be made. Cross-cultural similarity in the context of drastic differences in other aspects of the cultures is highly informative with regard to claims of universality. An example of a study that explored cross-cultural similarities in widely different groups (Dutch and illiterate Juang subjects) has been reported by Poortinga (1993).

Sampling of Subjects

Suppose that one is interested in comparing spatial reasoning among adolescents in several cultures. Within each culture we could take a random sample of the population (let us not consider the cost and effort involved). When we have an appropriate measure of the construct, simple random sampling will enable a comparison of average levels of spatial reasoning in each country. Yet simple random sampling is often of limited utility in cross-cultural research. In a study of highly dissimilar groups it may be desirable to adopt a sampling scheme that allows us to control for at least some of the cultural differences. When simple random sampling has been applied, it is hard to conclude whether the cultural differences observed are due to valid cultural differences or to noncontrolled differences (e.g., education, demographic characteristics). Therefore, the study could be carried out among groups that are as similar as possible on relevant background variables. This is called stratified random sampling.

Two strategies are often used to control for demographic differences across cultural groups. First, *matching* of subjects can be applied; the samples of the cultural groups to be compared are made as similar as possible in their demographic characteristics. Only subjects that fit a certain demographic profile will be sampled for the study. College students from different cultures are often compared, and it is assumed that their demographic characteristics are similar across cultures. In a similar vein, Hofstede (1980, 1983) obtained a sample of employees of a single multinational organization in 53 countries and was able to argue that the subjects were similar in their demographic characteristics across the nations studied. Schwartz (1992, 1994) sampled secondary school teachers from various countries (in addition to students) to maximize the comparability of his subjects.

It is sometimes difficult to employ a matching strategy because of constraints in resources and subject availability, or because the cultural groups being compared are sharply different in their demographic profiles. The approach of *statistical control* can then be used, which requires the measurement of the major demographic variables upon which the cultural groups vary. These demographic variables are treated as covariates and controlled for when cultural comparisons are made (see Chapter 4, External Validation).

In our opinion, it is unfortunate that many cross-cultural studies ignore sample differences across cultures and fail to assess the impact of such differences on their results. Their conclusions may not hold in cross-validations. As a rule, if there is suspicion that the samples are different on some demographic variables, these variables should be measured and their impact assessed.

Procedure

In this section we will present an overview of the most important and frequently encountered problems and remedies suggested in the administration of instruments in a cross-cultural context (see Lonner & Berry, 1986; van de Vijver & Poortinga, 1992). The description is based on a differentiation among five problem areas: tester/interviewer, testee/interviewee, interaction between these two, response procedures, and stimulus materials.

The obtrusiveness of the person of the *tester/interviewer* is a potential source of problems. The mere presence of a culturally different person can strongly affect respondents' behavior; for example, the presence of an experimenter may influence mother-child interactions (Super, 1981). To overcome the problem, the tester or a data collection device such as a video camera or decoy can be set up for an advance period before data collection begins. Several empirical studies have addressed the obtrusiveness of the tester's culture on the assessed IQ of the respondents. Jensen (1980) has reviewed the evidence and concludes that most of the studies suffer from methodological problems such as a nonrandom assignment of respondents to testers. The few methodologically accurate studies did not show a major effect of tester. Unfortunately, the generalizability of Jensen's study is limited, dealing only with intelligence tests in the United States. There has also been social-psychological and sociological research on interviewer effects. Cotter, Cohen, and Coulter (1982) found some evidence for a theory of deference: Subjects were more likely to display positive attitudes to a particular cultural group when they are interviewed by someone from that group (see Reese, Danielson, Shoemaker, Chang, & Hsu, 1986). In general, however, the size of interviewer effects tends to be small and inconsistent across studies (Singer & Presser, 1989).

There are two ways to deal with tester effects: a priori and a posteriori techniques. Examples of the former are the establishment of inter-viewer-interviewee acquaintance and the training of interviewers to alert them to the problem. An a posteriori technique is the measurement of tester characteristics. In studies involving many interviewers, their characteristics may be measured in order to enable, if needed, a statis-tical correction for these characteristics. For example, interviewers' age and attitudes can be used as covariates in an analysis of covariance. As usual in cross-cultural research, a priori and a posteriori techniques are complementary and cannot replace each other; a covariance analysis as suggested cannot make up for poor interviewer training and data collection.

Sample differences may pose another type of problem of administra-tion. Cross-cultural studies often involve highly dissimilar groups. Consequently, groups can differ in many background characteristics, only some of which are relevant to the topic studied. Differential expe-riences with cognitive tests and with measurement situations are exam-ples of performance-related, though usually unwanted, sources of cross-cultural variation. A Likert-type scale format that requires the expression of attitudes, opinions, and feelings on an ordinal or interval scale may have a low ecological validity in some cultures.

Prior and post hoc remedies can be envisaged to alleviate problems of sample incomparability. Examples of prior procedures are the use of lengthy instructions including various examples and exercises, and the application of an instrument in a pilot study in a nonstandard way. For instance, the instrument is administered to a member of the target group by a researcher or an interpreter with the aim of examining the instru-ment instead of gathering data about the respondent. All kinds of questions are asked of the respondent to establish whether he or she answers the intended questions in a meaningful way. The respondent can be asked for his or her interpretation of an item or the reason for the answer given. When this procedure has been followed for a few respon-dents, it will help to identify weaknesses in the instrument. Finally, a cross-cultural comparison of gain patterns obtained in repeated testing procedures can yield information on the presence of bias. When subjects with equal levels at the pretest from different cultural groups show dissimilar gain patterns at the posttest, there is strong evidence for the inequivalence of scores in both groups at the pretest.

Problems due to sample incomparability can sometimes be alleviated by a careful choice of samples. Thus, in the Vygotskian tradition, literacy is taken to have a formative influence on abstract thinking. Studies of the adequacy of the theory are troubled by the confounding of literacy and schooling: Comparisons between literates and illiterates are, almost by definition, comparisons between schooled and unschooled individuals. Scribner and Cole (1981) solved the problem of confounding by studying literacy among the Vai in Liberia. In this group a script is used that is not transmitted through formal education but through education in an informal setting, called "unschooled literacy" by the authors. A comparison of schooled literates and unschooled literates circumvents the confounding of schooling and literacy. The Cree, Native Americans living in Canada, also teach their indigenous script in informal settings (Berry & Bennett, 1991). Among both the Vai and the Cree, strong evidence was found for a limited influence of literacy on abstract thinking. It was found that the often observed, broad cognitive differences between schooled and unschooled individuals cannot be accounted for by literacy.

Post hoc procedures entail the measurement of and statistical correction for relevant background characteristics. Thus, van de Vijver (1988, 1991) administered tests of inductive thinking to primary and secondary school children in Zambia, Turkey, and the Netherlands and found that measures of school quality could statistically explain observed cross-cultural differences among the groups.

Tester-testee/interviewer-interviewee interaction can also give rise to administration problems. Unambiguous communication is a prerequisite for adequate instrument use across cultures. There is a rich literature on cross-cultural communication containing many examples of miscommunications (e.g., Asante & Gudykunst, 1989). An example of a communication failure in cross-cultural studies can be found in the work of Greenfield (1966). She studied Piagetian conservation among unschooled Wolof children. Two uncolored glass beakers of equal size are filled with an equal amount of water. One of the beakers is then poured into a third beaker that is smaller and broader than the others. The subject is asked which beaker contains more water. Nonconservers will typically say that the taller beaker has more water in it. Greenfield reported much nonconservation among the Wolof, even among 12-year-olds, an age at which most Western children would give the correct answer. Irvine (1978), replicating Greenfield's work, argued that the question of which beaker has more water is ambiguous in the Wolof language, because "more" can refer both to the amount and the level of the water. When this communication ambiguity was resolved by using different wording, Irvine found a higher level of conservation.

The literature on cross-cultural communication provides various a priori techniques on how to improve communication accuracy. When interviewers and interviewees have a different cultural background, interviewers will not only need to learn how to administer the interview, but they should also be skilled in intercultural communication (Asante & Gudykunst, 1989). This is a broad term encompassing, among other things, openness and clarity in communication; an ability to assume an interviewee's viewpoint; and an inviting, nonevaluative tone of interviewing (Hammer, 1989).

Post hoc procedures to assess the influence of communication accuracy have never been applied in cross-cultural research, although it is easy to do so. When measures of interviewers' communication skills or of the interview quality are available, they can be used as covariates in an analysis of covariance.

Response procedures can be another source of administration problems. Serpell's (1979) study, in which patterns were copied using iron wire and paper and pencil, illustrates the relevance of familiarity of response procedures (see Chapter 2, Method Bias). A well-known, a priori method for examining the influence of response procedures is the application of a monotrait-multimethod matrix, as in Serpell's study. The response is measured in more than one medium and results are compared across media (see Chapter 3, Validity Enhancement in Assessment, for other examples). A comparison will amount to the computation of cross-cultural differences in the two media as measured by their effect size (defined as the absolute difference of the means in two groups, divided by their pooled standard deviation). Dissimilar effect sizes point to the influence of response procedures. A posteriori techniques can also be applied. Subjects can be asked to rate their familiarity with the response procedure(s) applied (e.g., frequency of previous exposure) and a statistical correction for cross-cultural differences in familiarity can be carried out in an analysis of covariance.

The last source of administration problems, *stimulus characteristics*, has been most widely examined and documented, particularly in the area of mental testing. Differential stimulus familiarity is an almost ubiquitous alternative hypothesis in comparisons between Western and non-Western individuals on cognitive tests (e.g., Deregowski & Serpell's, 1971, study on the sorting behavior of Scottish and Zambian children discussed in Chapter 2, Method Bias). The a priori and a posteriori techniques for studying differential response familiarity can also be applied to stimulus familiarity. Regrettably, a systematic variation of stimuli and response media is rarely applied in cross-cultural studies. Comparisons of Western and non-Western individuals on cognitive tests, commonly derived from Western cultures, will become more interpretable if they are based on a systematic variation of stimulus and response formats. This will be further explored in the next section.

Validity Enhancement

This section describes measures that can be taken to enhance the validity in two areas of cross-cultural research: multilingual studies (translation of instruments) and assessment (measurement procedures).

Validity Enhancement in Multilingual Studies

Cross-cultural researchers frequently apply instruments in different languages in a study. Procedures to arrive at translations that are equivalent from a psychological perspective and methods for the evaluation of equivalence are described in this section (see Bracken & Barona, 1991; Brislin, 1980; Hambleton, 1994; Vallerand, 1989; van de Vijver & Hambleton, 1996). Most multilingual studies use instruments that were developed for a single language and cultural setting (successive development); only in a small number of studies are instruments simultaneously developed in at least two linguistic groups. There will be some emphasis on successive development in our discussion because of its prevalence.

Three options are available in multilingual studies. First, an instrument can be *applied*, in which case a literal translation is taken to be linguistically and psychologically appropriate in all groups studied. The literature contains many examples of the application option. Smith, Tisak, Bauman, and Green (1991) studied the equivalence of a translated circadian rhythm questionnaire in English and Japanese. Several discrepancies between the original and translated scales were found.

Second, an instrument can be *adapted* for use in a different cultural context. Instrument adaptation amounts to the literal translation of a set of items and a change in wording or contents of other items in order to enhance their appropriateness in the new cultural context. Examples of instrument adaptations are not numerous, despite the frequently observed need to apply this method (e.g., Berry, Poortinga, Segall, & Dasen, 1992; Brislin, 1986; Geisinger, 1994). An example can be found in the work of Lucio, Reyes-Lagunes, and Scott (1994). These authors adapted the Minnesota Multiphasic Personality Inventory (MMPI) for Mexico. Some items were translated literally, whereas others were adapted to the local context.

The statistical analyses in instrument adaptations often amount to the establishment of construct equivalence of the original and adapted instrument. For instance, Cheung (1989), who adapted the MMPI to China, provides evidence for the validity of the scale by examining its ability to discriminate between normals and patients and by computing profiles for different diagnostic groups. She reported patterns similar to those found in the United States. As another example, Liu et al. (1994) adapted the Cognitive Abilities Screening Instrument, an instrument developed in the United States, to diagnose dementia in a Chinese population with a low level of formal education. Another example of an adaptation is Spielberger, Gorsuch, and Lushene's (1970) State-Trait Anxiety Inventory. The instrument has been adapted to more than 40 languages. The various language versions are not literal translations of the English-language original; rather, the inventories were adapted in such a way that the underlying constructs, state and trait anxiety, were measured adequately in each language.

The third option is called *assembly*. In this case the original instrument is assumed to be inadequate in a new context (e.g., because of inappropriate item content) and a new instrument is developed to capture the construct more adequately in the new cultural context. Ho's (1996) study of filial piety discussed in Chapter 1, under Cross-Cultural Studies as Quasi-Experiments, illustrates this approach. Serpell's (1993) study of the local conceptualization of intelligence of individuals in Zambia and the composition of a test on the basis of this conceptualization is another example. In the personality area, Church's (1987) work can be mentioned. In his view, Western personality instruments do not cover indigenous personality constructs of the Filipino culture. He formulated directions for the construction of a culturally more appropriate personality instrument. Finally, Cheung et al. (1996) argued that adapting a Western personality measure would not capture all relevant dimensions of personality in the Chinese culture. They have developed the Chinese Personality Assessment Inventory, which contains several indigenous personality dimensions such as "face" and "harmony."

The first option, application, is by far the least cumbersome choice. Compared to the other options, application requires the least effort and money, best preserves the possibility of a high level of equivalence, and most easily allows for direct comparisons with results by others using the same instrument. Despite these advantages, it is easy to find examples in which such a procedure is inadequate. For instance, it was argued before that the characteristic behaviors or attitudes associated with constructs may differ across cultures, as was found for filial piety (see Chapter 1, Cross-Cultural Studies as Quasi-Experiments). Construct inequivalence renders direct applications inappropriate.

The major criterion in the choice of application, adaptation, and assembly is the type of bias expected. If there are serious concerns that construct bias (as in the example of filial piety) could play a role, adaptation or assembly should be chosen. Indigenization (Sinha, 1997), which aims at maximizing the appropriateness of psychological theories and instruments to local cultures, will often amount to the assembly of new instruments. These options can also be chosen when literal translation would lead to method bias. When only a few items are expected to show cultural idiosyncrasies, however, the composition of an entirely new instrument is superfluous and will unnecessarily limit the opportunities of cross-cultural comparison. An adaptation of the instrument in which only the presumably biased items are replaced will suffice. When no construct and method bias are to be expected, a straightforward application of the translated instrument will often be preferred.

Linguistic considerations also play a role in evaluating the appropriateness of an instrument in a multilingual context. An important linguistic aspect is translatability (see Brislin, 1980, 1986; Brislin, Lonner, & Thorndike, 1973). A text is poorly translatable when the loss of salient characteristics cannot be avoided in translation. These characteristics include denotations, connotations, language-specific meaning that is derived from a particular grammatical structure, and so on. Examples of poorly translatable text features are idiomatics (e.g., Spencer, 1988) and metaphors (e.g., Dunnigan, McNall, & Mortimer, 1993). Local idiom, which is often used in instruments that were originally intended for monolingual usage only, has a combination of conciseness and clarity that is often difficult to transfer to other languages.

Brislin (1986, pp. 143-150) has formulated a set of guidelines for writing new items and modifying existing ones. The guidelines are aimed at optimizing the translatability of items. These are summarized here:

1. Use short, simple sentences of fewer than 16 words.
2. Employ the active rather than the passive voice, because the former is easier to comprehend.
3. Repeat nouns instead of using pronouns, because the latter may have vague referents; in English, for example, *you* can refer to any number of persons.
4. Avoid metaphors and colloquialisms.
5. Avoid the subjunctive form, with words like *could* and *would*. Many languages express this meaning in different ways, thereby putting a burden on the translator.
6. Add sentences to provide context for key ideas. Redundancy is not harmful for communicating key aspects of the instrument.
7. Avoid verbs and prepositions telling "where" and "when" that do not have a definite meaning. How many times a week do you have to see someone in order to say that you see him "often"?
8. Avoid possessive forms where possible, because it may be difficult to determine the ownership. The ownership such as "his" in "his dog" has to be derived from the context of the sentence and languages do not have similar rules for expressing this ownership.
9. Use specific rather than general terms. Who is included in "members of your family" strongly differs across cultures; more precise terms are less likely to run into this problem.

Different procedures have been proposed to translate instruments. The most commonly applied is the translation-backtranslation procedure (Werner & Campbell, 1970). A text is translated from a source into a target language; a second interpreter (or group of interpreters) independently translates the text back into the source language. The accuracy of the translation is evaluated by comparing the original and backtranslated versions. Nontrivial differences between the versions are seen as pointing to translation problems. The procedure has been widely applied; it can identify various kinds of errors. Even when researchers have no command of the target language, the procedure provides them with a powerful tool for checking translation accuracy. Yet in our view, the procedure has a serious drawback: It puts a premium on literal translations, and such translations can yield a stilted language that does not approach the naturalness of the text in the original version. A translation-backtranslation procedure pays more attention to the semantics and less to connotations, naturalness, and comprehensibility. When translators know that their work will be evaluated by backtranslation, these problems become serious. A separate assessment of connotative aspects, naturalness, and comprehensibility may be required.

An interesting alternative for overcoming these problems is cultural decentering of the instrument (Werner & Campbell, 1970; see also Chapter 2, Levels of Equivalence). Its aim echoes the goals of the culture-free and culture-fair test movement. Cultural decentering amounts to the removal of words and concepts in a source language that are difficult to translate or are specific to a culture. So, an instrument in the source language is retrospectively changed in order to enhance its translatability. To some extent, problems arising from construct or method bias could be circumvented using decentering. A disadvantage of the approach is the amount of labor it requires. The preparation of the instrument presupposes a multicultural, multilingual team with expertise in the construct under study. Furthermore, data collected with the instrument in the source language before it was decentered cannot be used for cross-cultural comparisons. When the instrument has not been used before, cultural decentering amounts to the simultaneous development of an instrument in many languages. An example of this "simultaneous cultural decentering" can be found in the work of Tanzer, Gittler, and Ellis (1995). They developed a test of spatial ability that was used in Austria and the United States. The instructions and stimuli were simultaneously developed in German and English. An example of "successive cultural decentering" is not known to the authors. It may be noted that the term *decentering* is sometimes used to refer to measures to enhance the applicability of an instrument in a particular context (e.g., Cortese & Smyth, 1979). In the present terminology, this would be called *adaptation* because only the instrument in the target language is changed.

Another procedure for obtaining linguistically equivalent instruments involves a committee approach. Committees of bilinguals are asked to translate or adapt an instrument. When an adaptation is required, high demands will be placed on the psychological expertise of committee members. Large international boards such as the United Nations and the European Union rely on committees of bilinguals for translation. Some psychological studies also have used committees. It is not uncommon to combine the committee approach with translation-backtranslations, in which case independent committees take care of the translation and the backtranslation. The major strength of the committee approach is the cooperative effort, which can improve the quality of the translation, in particular when committee members have complementary areas of expertise. Some members may have more knowledge of the cultural background of speakers of the target language, while other members may have more expertise in the substantive aspects of the construct. A properly functioning committee can yield rigorous tests of the accuracy of the translation and/or adaptation. However, a disadvantage of the committee approach is the absence of an independent evaluation of the adequacy of the translation or adaptation. When a researcher does not speak the target language, he or she will need additional evidence to evaluate the quality of the committee's work.

An example of a committee approach was described by Bravo, Woodbury, Canino, and Rubio-Stipec (1993). These authors adapted the Diagnostic Interview Schedule for Children, a U.S. scale, for Puerto Rico. They followed a translation-backtranslation procedure using a committee of bilinguals. Committees of bilinguals are sometimes not involved in the translation but only in a check of the accuracy of the translation. Bracken and Fouad (1987) obtained a Spanish translation of the American Bracken Basic Concept Scale by iterations of translations and backtranslations, followed by an independent check by a committee of bilinguals. Similarly, Sperber, Devellis, and Boehlecke (1994) developed a translation of an American questionnaire of medical students' attitudes toward preventive medical services into Hebrew. Bilinguals were then asked to evaluate the accuracy of the translation independently.

The two procedures to obtain translations and adaptations, translation-backtranslation and the bilingual committee approach, use judgmental evidence to establish linguistic equivalence. These procedures are applied before the translated or adapted instrument is administered in a new linguistic context. In addition to judgmental procedures, statistical procedures have been proposed to check translation accuracy. Statistical procedures are usually based on empirical data obtained from the administration of an instrument to groups of monolinguals in each language or to bilinguals. Psychometric procedures usually compare item statistics obtained for the various linguistic versions. Dissimilar item statistics are taken to point to some kind of inequivalence, due either to poor translation, inadequate item content, or some valid difference on that particular item, between the groups studied. All techniques that have been proposed to examine item bias can also be used to assess linguistic equivalence. The techniques, discussed in detail in Chapter 4, Item Bias Analysis, are just briefly mentioned here. Item response theory (also discussed in Chapter 4, Item Bias Analysis, and Box 4.6) is a popular and flexible tool for studying linguistic equivalence. For instance, Ellis, Becker, and Kimmel (1993) used it to establish the equivalence of an English-language version of the Trier Personality Inventory and the original German version. Among the 120 items tested, 11 items were found to be biased. Bontempo (1993) developed French and Chinese versions of an English-language individualism-collectivism scale. He administered the instrument to students in France (in French), China and Hong Kong (in Chinese), and the United States (in English). Several items were found to be biased. Comparison of covariance structures has also been used to study linguistic equivalence. For instance, Cudeck and Claassen (1983) investigated the factorial equivalence of the New South African Group Test Intermediate Form G in Afrikaans and English. The covariance matrices of the subtests were compared for Afrikaans-speaking and English-speaking students (13 years of age). Evidence for factorial invariance was found. Finally, Peterson, Smith, and Tayeb (1993) studied the adequacy of performance and maintenance measures of leadership used for production employees in Japanese manufacturing organizations. The measures were translated from English into Japanese. Structural equation modeling showed some weaknesses in the measures.

Guidelines

A committee representing various international psychological organizations has recently formulated guidelines for translating and adapting psychological and educational instruments (Hambleton, 1994; van de Vijver & Hambleton, 1996). The present section summarizes the work of the committee. A total of 22 guidelines were formulated, covering four facets of multilingual studies: context (defining the general background), development and adaptation (recommended practices in designing multilingual instruments), administration (defining issues regarding instrument administrations), and documentation and score interpretation (defining issues in the interpretation and cross-cultural comparisons of scores). Each of the guidelines will be quoted, followed by a short explanation. The reader will find overlap between some guidelines and materials we have discussed. For reasons of completeness, however, we have chosen to describe all guidelines.

The guidelines on context are as follows:

---

1. *Effects of cultural differences that are not relevant or important to the main purposes of the study should be minimized to the extent possible.*

Multilingual studies should attempt to generate interpretable cross-cultural differences by eliminating as many sources of bias as possible. The guideline covers all stages of a multilingual study, from the formulation of the theoretical background to the writing of the final report. It is not stated that all relevant cross-cultural differences can be eliminated; instead, the more realistic position is adopted that every attempt should be made to minimize unwanted differences. For instance, in administering educational tests to pupils in countries with highly dissimilar school systems, it may be impossible to eliminate differential experience with educational tests. Yet a lengthy instruction with several examples and exercises and a careful choice of stimuli can reduce these differences considerably.

---

2. The amount of overlap in the constructs in the populations of interest should be assessed.

The distorting influence of construct bias is acknowledged in this guideline by positing that similarity of constructs cannot be assumed but should be assessed. The guideline will be particularly relevant when the construct studied is broad, such as intelligence, and when there is a large cultural distance between the groups studied (see Chapter 2, Construct Bias)

The guidelines on instrument development, translation, and adaptation are as follows:

---

3. Instrument developers/publishers should ensure that the translation/adaptation process takes full account of linguistic and cultural differences among the populations for whom the translated/adapted versions of the instrument are intended.

Translation is more than producing text in another language. Translators should know or be made aware of the linguistic and cultural differences that could influence responses to translated or adapted instruments. Hambleton (1994, p. 235) quotes an illustrative example. The following item was administered in a Swedish-English comparison of educational achievement:

Where is a bird with webbed feet most likely to live?
 a. in the mountains
 b. in the woods
 c. in the sea
 d. in the desert.

In the Swedish translation, "webbed feet" became "swimming feet." This translation gave a clear cue about the correct answer. Such unexpected and unintended item differences can lead to substantial performance differences across groups that may be erroneously attributed to differences in the underlying construct. Similarly, van de Vijver, Willemse, and Van de Rijt (1993), administering the WISC to native and migrant Dutch children, found that the question, *What is bacon?* was relatively difficult for migrant children. This is not surprising, because most of these children had an Islamic cultural background that has a food taboo on pork.

---

4. Instrument developers/publishers should provide evidence that the language use in the directions, rubrics, and items themselves as well as in the handbook are appropriate for all cultural and language populations for whom the instrument is intended.

Several Western instruments are inappropriate in a non-Western context because of problems with the wording of the instruction, examples, or test items such as long or unnecessarily complex sentences, the use of infrequent words, and the application of single or double negations (see Brislin's, 1986, recommendations on how to write translatable items given above).

---

5. Instrument developers/publishers should provide evidence that the testing techniques, item formats, test conventions, and procedures are familiar to all intended populations.

A high performance on psychological and educational instruments requires skills that are present in Western-educated groups, such as the ability to work individually on a task for a fairly long period of time and to make the subtle linguistic discriminations that are typically required in choosing between alternatives in multiple-choice items. Such skills have to be mastered. Individuals with a different cultural and educational background may not have an equal mastery of these skills. For example, the ability to strike a balance between speed and accuracy in speeded tests assumes previous exposure to similar instruments. Individuals without such experience may prefer extreme speed or extreme accuracy; in both cases a low score will result. Awareness among test developers/publishers of the crucial role of familiarity in assessment will enhance the validity of cross-cultural comparisons.

---

6. Instrument developers/publishers should
provide evidence that item content and stimulus
materials are familiar to all intended populations.

This guideline does not opt for the position that all stimulus materials should be equally familiar to all individuals concerned. A more realistic position is chosen, holding that stimuli should be familiar through previous experience or that they should be made familiar through a lengthy instruction.

That the role of stimulus familiarity is mentioned in a separate guideline is an acknowledgment of its vital importance, particularly in the area of cognitive and educational testing, where it can induce large performance differences across groups. A good example of studies in which stimulus familiarity needs careful scrutiny is formed by international comparisons of scholastic achievement. Problems should be framed in an equally familiar context; however, the adaptation of metrication and currency units to all countries involved can change the item difficulty. For instance, the numbers that are needed in making computations involving prices of daily commodities will differ between the United States and France because one U.S. dollar and one French franc differ considerably in value. As a consequence, quite different numbers are involved in computing the price for a number of units in the two places (e.g., seven loaves of bread).

---

7. Instrument developers/publishers should
implement systematic judgmental evidence, both
linguistic and psychological, to improve the accuracy
of the translation/adaptation process and compile
evidence on the equivalence of all language versions.

The guideline refers to standardized translation procedures (such as the use of translation-backtranslation and of committees of bilinguals) that were described previously in this section.

---

8. Instrument developers/publishers should ensure that the data collection design permits the use of appropriate statistical techniques to establish item equivalence between the different language versions of the instrument.

Various designs have been used to study differential item functioning to scrutinize translation accuracy. Hambleton (1994, pp. 237-238) mentions three: (a) bilinguals take the source and target versions of the instrument; (b) source-language monolinguals take the original and backtranslated versions; and (c) source-language monolinguals take the source language and target-language monolinguals take target-language versions. The latter is most frequently applied. Unfortunately, the design confounds group and instrument characteristics; a cross-cultural difference on a particular item can be due to poor translation (e.g., inadequate word choice) or to group characteristics (e.g., Groups A and B have a different standing on the construct underlying the item). These two interpretations can be disentangled by also studying the responses of bilinguals (as done in the first design).

---

9. Instrument developers/publishers should apply appropriate statistical techniques to (a) establish the equivalence of the different versions of the instrument and (b) identify problematic components or aspects of the instrument which may be inadequate to one or more of the intended populations.

In addition to the linguistic equivalence that was specified in Guideline 7, instrument developers/publishers should put forward statistical evidence to establish the psychometric equivalence of the instruments.

> *10. Instrument developers/publishers should
> provide information on the evaluation of
> validity in all target populations for whom the
> translated/adapted versions are intended.*

The need to establish measurement properties (such as reliability and validity) for each cultural group studied and to compare these properties across groups runs like a thread through the guidelines. Validity of translated or adapted instruments cannot be taken for granted but requires empirical verification; nomological networks of original and translated instruments may not be identical.

> *11. Instrument developers/publishers should
> provide statistical evidence of the equivalence
> of questions for all intended populations.*

Equivalence of translations can be statistically examined by the application of item bias techniques (to be discussed in Chapter 4 under Item Bias Analysis).

> *12. Nonequivalent questions between versions intended
> for different populations should **not** be used in preparing a
> common scale or in comparing these populations. However, they
> may be useful in enhancing content validity of scores reported
> for each population separately* (emphasis in original).

An item that is shown to be biased cannot be used for cross-cultural comparisons. Yet if such an item shows appropriate item characteristics in a cultural group (such as an adequate fit to an item response model), there is no reason to discard the item in that group; it may add to the construct and predictive validity of the instrument.

The guidelines on administration are as follows:

---

13. Instrument developers and administrators
should try to anticipate the types of problems
that can be expected and take appropriate actions
to remedy these problems through the preparation
of appropriate materials and instructions.

Administration problems are not often unexpected. Several problems can be anticipated and remedied by appropriate instrument design. A small pilot study in which the instrument is administered in a nonstandard way can help to identify these problems (see above, Procedure).

---

14. Instrument administrators should be sensitive to
a number of factors related to the stimulus materials,
administration procedures, and response modes that can
moderate the validity of the inferences drawn from the scores.

Instrument administrators should be aware of aspects of instruments that can create problems during the administration, such as particular examples or uncommon words in the instruction. Some of these aspects will be specific to the instrument. Particularly when they start working with the instrument and have not yet built up their own experience, test administrators can benefit from a description in the manual of validity-moderating factors. Other factors are of a more global nature, such as working with speeded tests or communicating about intimate issues when the interviewer and interviewee do not know each other.

---

15. Those aspects of the environment that
influence the administration of an instrument
should be made as similar as possible across
populations for whom the instrument is intended.

The guideline refers to physical conditions. In field research it may be difficult to achieve similar conditions for subjects in all groups. It is difficult to make the physical conditions similar in well-equipped Western schools and poorly equipped schools in Third World countries. Still, it is important to attempt to equate conditions as much as possible (see Chapter 2, Method Bias).

> *16. Instrument administration instructions*
> *should be in the source and target languages to*
> *minimize the influence of unwanted sources*
> *of variation across populations.*

Unwanted sources of cross-cultural variation, such as differences in stimulus familiarity and familiarity of the testing or interview situation, can be minimized by providing many examples and exercises and by allotting sufficient time for instruction. A pretest session in which subjects can become acquainted with the testing or interview situation will also reduce cross-cultural differences in stimulus or response format familiarity.

> *17. The instrument manual should specify all aspects*
> *of the instrument and its administration that*
> *require scrutiny in the application of the*
> *instrument in a new cultural context.*

On the basis of their experience with the instrument, administrators will know which aspects of the instrument or its administration require special attention. For instance, some examples may be relatively difficult in a particular cultural group. A list of such features in the manual is helpful to colleagues who will administer the instrument. A well-known example is the Raven Coloured Progressive Matrices. The examples and the first part of the test can be solved using a perceptually based strategy. Subsequent items become much more analytical, however; the transition is not announced, nor can it be derived from the examples. It has been noted several times that subjects from cultural groups with little testing experience may become confused by the transition and be unable to answer the remaining items.

---

18. The administration should be unobtrusive, and the examiner-examinee interaction should be minimized. Explicit rules that are described in the manual for the instrument should be followed.

Extensive interaction between administrators and examinees should be discouraged in cross-cultural measurement because the tester/interviewer can introduce a nonstandardized and potentially important source of variation. It is therefore important to standardize the interaction to the extent possible and to explicitly describe the role of the administrator in the manual (see above, Procedure).

The guidelines on documentation/score interpretations are as follows:

---

19. When an instrument is translated/adapted for use in another population, documentation of the changes should be provided, along with evidence of the equivalence.

Colleagues who consider applying an instrument in the new cultural context need information on its adequacy. A documentation of features that were included to enhance the instrument's appropriateness in different cultural contexts and a report of results of equivalence studies are convenient aids for evaluating its appropriateness.

---

*20. Score differences among samples of populations administered the instrument should **not** be taken at face value. The researcher has the responsibility to substantiate the differences with other empirical evidence* (emphasis in original).

The guideline is in line with the general theme of this book: that cross-cultural score differences on psychological instruments should not be taken for granted and that additional empirical evidence is required to interpret these differences. The guideline puts the burden of proof on the researcher instead of, say, instrument users, the scientific community, or journal editors. The approach may seem restrictive, but it forms a sound policy against the formulation of sweeping, ill-founded statements about cross-cultural differences that abound in the history of cross-cultural research.

---

21. Comparisons across populations can only be made at the level of invariance that has been established for the scale on which scores are reported.

Without an explicit examination of equivalence, no claims can be made about cross-cultural differences and similarities. In the past there have been too many studies in which a Western instrument was translated and applied in a non-Western group, and the difference in average group scores was then tested for significance without any check of translation accuracy, appropriateness of the instrument in the new context, and equivalence of the scores. Much of past research worked from the assumption that instruments yielded scalar equivalence until the opposite was shown (e.g., in the form of item bias). In contrast, the present guideline works from the assumption that scores can be compared only when their equivalence has been demonstrated.

---

22. The instrument developer should provide specific information on the ways in which the sociocultural and ecological contexts of the populations might affect performance on the instrument and should suggest procedures to account for these effects in the interpretation of results.

An instrument developer may often have collected information on the influence of various background factors such as gender, age, and education. Users of the instrument should be notified of such effects and of ways to account for them.

TABLE 3.1   Overview of Techniques to Enhance the Validity of
Cross-Cultural Assessment

When Implemented?	Technique
Before data collection	Adaptation or assembly of instruments
	Development of new instruments
	Repeated test administration
	Triangulation
	Experimental control of context variables
After data collection	Item bias analysis
	Application of differential norms

Validity Enhancement in Assessment

Assessment is an important aspect of virtually all cross-cultural research. A recurrent complaint in the literature is the often poor level of appropriateness of Western measures in cross-cultural research. Notably, cross-cultural psychologists have a long tradition of discussing the problems of the use of Western instruments in non-Western settings (e.g., Irvine & Carroll, 1980; Schwarz, 1961). The reasons for the problems are quickly appreciated when one has struggled or seen someone struggling with administering an instrument that is culturally alien to the respondent. At least four types of modifications have been proposed to enhance the validity of instruments in a cross-cultural context (see Helms-Lorenz & van de Vijver, 1995). Although most types have been developed in the context of ability and aptitude testing, they extend to other types of assessment. Issues in assessment in cross-cultural counseling have been discussed by Dana (1993), Lonner and Ibrahim (1996), Paniagua (1994), and Sodowski and Impara (1996).

All validity-enhancing procedures start from the premise that observed differences between cultural groups are open to multiple interpretations and that additional measures should be taken to rule out as many alternative explanations as possible. The techniques can be grouped as a priori and a posteriori procedures, depending on whether they are applied before or after data collection on some target variables (see Table 3.1).

Various a priori techniques have been developed to enhance the validity of cross-cultural assessment, some of which implement changes in the instrument whereas others are related to the design of the study. To start with the former, we have discussed three options in instrument translation: application, adaptation, and assembly (previous section). When the presumed impact of bias is low, a literal translation and *application* of the instrument in the new context is a good choice. If the impact of construct and method bias is assumed to be present though not yet so large as to invalidate the whole instrument, measures can be *adapted* in order to increase their expediency. When there are salient cross-cultural differences in the conceptualization of the construct studied, it may be necessary to *assemble* an entirely new instrument. The assembly of new instruments, very infrequently reported in the literature, can take two forms. First, one can develop a culture-specific instrument. Such an assembly will inevitably lead to a low level of equivalence of scores because each cultural group has its own version of the instrument; when there is only a small overlap in the construct across cultural groups, it is unrealistic to assume equivalence in the scores.

Second, new measurement procedures can be designed to reduce shortcomings of existing instruments (especially method bias). The idea of using the same instrument in all cultural groups is not abandoned here; the aim is to design an instrument that is adequate for all relevant cultural groups. Two examples, derived from the domain of cognitive testing, are mentioned here. Both examples are meant as alternatives to the use of classical intelligence tests in multicultural groups. Traditional instruments rely heavily on knowledge of the local language and culture, which is an undesirable property when such knowledge is not available to the same extent among all cultural groups under study (assuming that this knowledge is not the topic of the study). The first alternative is the use of learning potential tests. The tests purportedly tap skills that are relevant for future learning; they place little reliance on knowledge gained in the past. Learning potential tests usually measure reasoning (inductive and deductive thinking) and memory (e.g., Hamers, Sijtsma, & Ruijssenaars, 1993; Lidz, 1987). Unlike conventional intelligence testing, the administration allows for help to be offered to the child in a standardized way. Such coaching can alleviate problems met by individuals with little or no relevant test experience. The flexibility of administration procedure adds to the relevance of learning potential tests in a multicultural setting. However, empirical work in the Netherlands has shown that despite all efforts to avoid explicit and implicit references to the Dutch society in the test, the test scores of migrant children are related to the length of their stay in the Netherlands. The explanation of this observation could well be that the test scores are influenced by knowledge of the Dutch language and culture and that the tests do not measure learning potential in a context-free manner.

The second alternative is based on an observation in experimental psychology that choice reaction times increase in a predictable manner with the number of alternatives and that this increase is related to intelligence test scores (e.g., Vernon, 1987). Various simple cognitive measures (such as choice reaction times) have been studied in their relationship with more complex cognitive measures. The potential relevance of simple cognitive tasks is obvious: They deal with simple, typically nonverbal stimuli that, compared to most paper-and-pencil tests, should be less affected by cultural background. van de Vijver and Willemse (1991) composed a battery of choice reaction time tasks of increasing complexity. The easiest task was a simple reaction time test. As one of the most difficult tasks, the pupil had to find the unmatched square in a set of five squares presented on a computer screen; the set consisted of two pairs of identical figures and an unmatched square (see Figure 3.1). Primary school pupils could complete all tasks with very few errors. However, the interest is not in the accuracy but in the speed of responding. No differences in average reaction times were found between native and migrant Dutch pupils from the highest grade of primary school; interestingly, reaction times were significantly correlated with school performance in both groups.

In addition to changes in the instrument, *design adaptations* are an important tool for reducing the number of alternative interpretations of observed cross-cultural differences. One possible adaptation involves the measurement of context variables, which is an effective means to corroborate a particular interpretation of cross-cultural differences (see Chapter 1, Cross-Cultural Studies as Quasi-Experiments). For example, the hypothesis that cross-cultural differences in cognitive test scores are related to education could be validated by measuring background variables related to education at individual (e.g., educational history), school (e.g., available learning materials), or national (e.g., per capita expenditure on education) level.

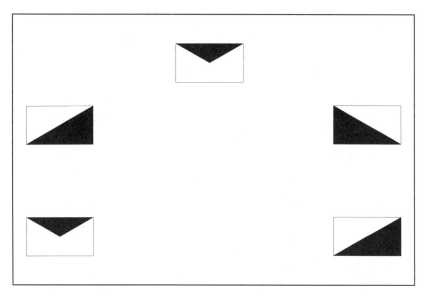

Figure 3.1. Example of Stimulus Display With Figural Stimuli Used in the Choice Reaction Time Experiment

Other design adaptations include repeated test administrations (in order to compare score changes across cultural groups; the procedure is particularly useful in the case of mental tests), the assessment of social desirability of the items of the instrument, and pilot studies to examine possibly precarious aspects of the instrument and its administration.

Triangulation can be seen as an application of the monotrait-multi-method approach; it involves the use of multiple, diverse measures to capture the same construct. This approach is especially useful in situations where statistical techniques for detecting biases do not apply, such as in the case of single-item measures (e.g., measures of social behavior and measures in Piagetian psychology). The logic underlying this approach is that if convergent results are obtained with different measures, bias is not likely to have produced the results. For instance, Hess, Chang, and McDevitt (1987) found that in comparison with American mothers, Chinese mothers were more likely to attribute the academic performance of their children to effort. Consistent with this result, Chinese children were also more likely to attribute their academic performance to their own effort than were American children.

The convergence between the results of children and mothers strengthened the validity of the cultural difference observed. In contrast, Serpell's (1979) study of Zambian and Scottish children's copying skills using iron-wire models and pencil drawing is an example of nonconvergent results.

Another interesting design adaptation is the *experimental manipulation of context variables* in order to assess their effects on cultural differences. This approach can illustrate the role of the context variables directly. For instance, Morris, Leung, and Sethi (1995) studied preferences for conflict resolution procedures in the United States and Hong Kong. Consistent with previous findings, Morris et al. found that Chinese preferred the use of mediation to resolve a dispute more than Americans did. Yet when the other disputant was described as hostile and emotionally unstable, cultural differences in the preference for mediation disappeared. This finding suggests that the preference of Chinese for mediation may be related to their implicit assumption that the other disputant is likely to be cooperative, and that Americans do not share this implicit assumption.

Another example of this approach is given by Cohen and Nisbett (Cohen & Nisbett, 1994; Cohen, Nisbett, Bowdle, & Schwarz, 1995; Nisbett, 1993). Their program of research attempts to explain why homicide rates are higher in the South than in the North in the United States. The basic argument is that in the Southern region, a "culture of honor" exists that requires men to maintain their reputation of toughness by responding violently to people who insult them. To provide support for this argument, Cohen et al. (1995) conducted an experiment in which they manipulated the occurrence of an insult. In the control condition in which an insult was absent, Southern and Northern subjects did not show any difference in their aggressiveness and violent behavior. In the experimental condition, an insult was experimentally introduced, and the reactions of Southern and Northern subjects were assessed. It was found that in this condition, Southern subjects were more likely to think that their masculine reputation was damaged by the insult, were more upset by the insult, and were more likely to display aggressive behavior. These findings provide evidence for the culture of honor as an explanation for the difference in violence between the North and the South in the United States.

In the studies by Morris et al. (1995) and Cohen et al. (1995), the explanatory variable was experimentally manipulated and its effects on subjects assessed. It should be noted that because it is not possible to assign subjects randomly to different experimental conditions in both cases, the experiments conducted are not true experiments. Still, the effects of the experimental manipulation of the context variable provide strong support for the mechanisms proposed for explaining the cultural differences observed. Obviously, this strategy can be applied only to context variables that can be experimentally manipulated and not to variables that are person-linked, such as education level.

The most important a posteriori technique in validity enhancement is *item bias analysis*. Linguistic and statistical analyses of the responses in an item bias analysis can be utilized to detect anomalous items (see Chapter 4, Item Bias Analysis).

A final procedure to enhance the validity of assessment in cross-cultural research entails the application of *differential norms* in order to enhance the fairness and accuracy of the decisions based on the test results. Whereas bias was located at item level in the previous approach, differential norms locate bias at the level of test scores: Similar scores obtained by individuals from different cultures may have a different meaning. In the area of selection and placement, differential norms are popular. Pass-fail decisions tend to be dependent on group membership. Differential norms are usually introduced to correct for social inequality and unequal opportunities in society for various cultural groups. Differential norms can take on a variety of forms; Petersen and Novick (1976) give an overview. In quota hiring, for instance, the proportion of applicants to be hired from each cultural group is agreed upon prior to the selection procedure. It is the task of the selection officer to select the best applicants from each group. As an alternative, in an "equal marginal risk" model the person with the lowest score from each group that is hired has the same probability of success in the job. The model produces the largest number of successful workers (see Cronbach, 1984, p. 389). There has been much debate as to whether regression lines predicting job success from psychological instruments are identical for Blacks and Whites in the United States. Schmidt and Hunter (1977; Hunter, Schmidt, & Hunter, 1979; see also Cronbach, 1984) have provided extensive empirical evidence pointing to the equality of regression lines for Blacks and Whites. This equality is often taken as evidence for the fairness of results. However, the evidence would be more persuasive if it were supported by an examination of the equivalence of both predictor and criterion scores for all cultural groups. Such an examination is hardly ever reported.

Differential grading and treatment of test scores is probably more widely applied in education than in any other institution. As an example, a nationwide achievement test is administered at the end of primary school in the Netherlands. The test scores, together with a teacher's judgment of the pupil's capacities, provide the basis for the teacher to advise the parents of the pupil about what type of secondary school may be most appropriate. There is evidence that migrants and natives with the same scores on the achievement test will often not receive the same advice. With similar test scores for natives and migrants, the latter are advised to seek an intellectually more demanding type of school (De Jong, 1987). The differential norms applied by the teachers are not based on explicit selection models such as described above but reflect tacitly employed models. Teachers appear to think that test scores of migrants underestimate their educational aptitudes and that test scores should be interpreted accordingly.

We conclude with a caveat. Validity-enhancing procedures can go a long way toward reducing problems of cross-cultural assessment. However, their implementation will not guarantee bias-free measurement. For example, new procedures may not meet their own goals, such as context-free measurement; the application of item bias techniques will not preclude construct bias. Finally, triangulation can only provide information about the rank ordering of cultures and does not guarantee scalar equivalence even when convergence is obtained. If Culture A scores higher than Culture B on several measures tapping the same construct, we are confident that the difference between the two cultures is valid. Yet we are still unable to quantify the magnitude of the cultural difference because the equality of the origin and the unit of the measurement scale across the two cultures are not assessed in triangulation.

4

Analysis

Data analysis in cross-cultural research involves more than the preparation of the correct instructions to run a computer program of a statistical package. It is a link in the long chain of empirical research that starts with the specification of a theoretical framework and ends with drawing conclusions. Strategic decisions in the data analysis, such as the choice of statistical techniques, can be made only on the basis of a combination of substantive considerations such as the research questions or hypotheses involved and statistical considerations such as measurement level and sample size.

The analysis of cross-cultural data often consists of two stages. The psychometric adequacy of an instrument, such as the computation of its reliability and item statistics (e.g., item-total correlations and item means and variances to check for floor or ceiling effects), is examined in the first part. The occurrence of item bias can also be probed. These preliminary analyses are discussed in the next section, Preliminary Analyses. The second stage of data analysis addresses the main issues of a study: the exploration of research questions or the testing of

BOX 4.1
Testing the Equality of
Reliability Coefficients in Two Groups

The statistic to test the equality of two independent reliability coefficients is $(1 - \alpha_1)/(1 - \alpha_2)$, in which α_1 and α_2 represent the reliabilities (usually Cronbach's α) of an instrument in two cultural groups. For large samples, the statistic follows an F distribution with $N_1 - 1$ and $N_2 - 1$ degrees of freedom (N_1 and N_2 are the sample sizes).

As an example, suppose that a test of 10 items has been administered to 250 subjects in each of two cultural groups and Cronbach's αs were .60 and .80, respectively. The above statistic is equal to $(1 - .60)/(1 - .80) = 2.00$, which is larger than the critical F ratio of 1.28 ($df_1 = df_2 = 249$) at $p = .05$ (two-tailed). So, it can be concluded that the reliability is significantly higher in the second group.

hypotheses. In our presentation we will make a distinction between structure-oriented statistical techniques and level-oriented statistical techniques. The application of external validation techniques using context variables is then described, followed by hierarchical linear models (multilevel analyses).

Preliminary Analyses

Traditional Psychometric Analysis

Cross-cultural comparisons of scores presuppose accurate psychometric properties of the measures in all groups. Preliminary analyses examine these properties at the item or instrument level. In the latter case, it is common to compare reliability coefficients. Equality of (independently obtained) reliability coefficients can be easily tested as illustrated in Box 4.1. If significant differences are observed (which is not common), their source should be scrutinized. Such differences can be produced by small sets of aberrant items that show floor or ceiling effects in one of the groups or do not measure the same construct in all groups. The latter can also be detected by comparing item-total corre-

TABLE 4.1 Item-Total Correlations of Fictitious Data Obtained in
Three Cultural Groups

Item	Group A	Group B	Group C
1	.27	.00	.10
2	.35	−.11	.15
3	.25	.38	.20
4	.40	.33	.20
5	.36	.41	.25
6	.43	.42	.25
7	.36	.42	.35
8	.25	.31	.30
9	.34	.33	.20
10	.24	.24	.28

lations across groups, as illustrated in the comparison between Group A and Group B in Table 4.1. The first two items of the measure have a lower item-total correlation in the second group than in the first group (.27 and .35 vs. .00 and −.11).

Differences in reliability coefficients could also be due to more global differences between the instruments. A comparison of item-total correlations of Culture A and C shows that most item-total correlations are lower in Culture C. Such lower values can result from various sources, such as lack of appropriateness of the instrument (e.g., construct inequivalence), administration problems (e.g., substantial interviewer effects or low interrater reliability), subject characteristics (e.g., cross-cultural differences in test-wiseness), and differential response styles (e.g., acquiescence or social desirability). Differences in the shape of the score distribution across groups that can be visually checked can also be relevant. Dissimilar forms may point to various problems of the instrument or its administration.

In sum, an examination of the psychometric characteristics of instruments is an important first step in the analysis of cross-cultural data. The analysis explores the quality of the data. Causes of cross-cultural differences need to be scrutinized. These traditional psychometric tools have at least two attractive properties: They are widely available in common statistical packages, and they do not require large sample sizes.

Item Bias Analysis

Definition

A host of statistically more rigorous alternatives to classical item-statistics has been proposed to identify anomalous items (e.g., Berk, 1982; Camilli & Shepard, 1994; Holland & Wainer, 1993; Shepard, Camilli, & Averill, 1981). They have become known as item bias or differential item functioning techniques. An item is an unbiased measure of a theoretical construct, say, dominance, if persons from different cultural groups who are equally dominant have the same average score on the item. In more formal terms, persons with an equal standing on the theoretical construct underlying the instrument should have the same expected score on the item, irrespective of group membership. The expression "with an equal standing" is essential in the definition. The definition of bias does not stipulate that the averages of the cultural groups should be identical, but only that these averages should be identical across cultural groups for persons who are equally dominant. By specifying that item scores should have the same average for persons with the same standing on the underlying construct, we can distinguish between valid differences and bias. Nobody would want to argue that all observed cross-cultural differences point to bias; we would not want to confound valid cross-cultural differences (often called "impact") and bias. A schematic overview of item bias detection techniques is given in Box 4.2.

Item Bias Detection in Numerical Scores

We will illustrate three methods to identify bias. The first is an extension of Cleary and Hilton's (1968) use of analysis of variance, a technique for interval- and ratio-level data. The second is the Mantel-Haenszel statistic, presently the most popular item bias method for dichotomous data. Finally, we will illustrate how item response theory can be used to examine item bias.

Suppose that a questionnaire of twenty 5-point items (scores: 1-5) has been administered to 500 members of Culture A and 500 members of Culture B. The Likert-type scores will be treated here as interval variables. Item bias is examined use an analysis of variance. Bias is examined for each item separately. The item score is the dependent variable, while cultural group (2 levels) and score levels are the independent variables. We call this analysis of variance conditional because score level is used in the design specification as an independent variable (the distinction between conditional and unconditional techniques is further explained in Box 4.2).

Score groups are almost always composed on the basis of the total score on the instrument (i.e., the sum of the item scores). The minimum score on our questionnaire is $20 \times 1 = 20$ and the maximum score is $20 \times 5 = 100$. The minimum and maximum score groups will not be considered, because the responses of all persons would necessarily be identical across all cultural groups. In these groups bias cannot be studied. The remaining 79 score groups $(21, 22, 23, \ldots, 99)$ provide useful information for item bias analysis. In real studies it is usually impossible to separate all possible score groups for the obvious reason that several if not most of the levels will have insufficient data to warrant such an analysis. In our example, 500 persons are distributed across 79 score levels. A split in all score levels will result in level groups with few or even no subjects. As a consequence, we will have to concatenate score levels. There is an important trade-off to keep in mind in determining the appropriate number of score levels. A larger number of levels will allow for a more fine-grained and a statistically more powerful analysis of item bias (Clauser, Mazor, & Hambleton, 1994), but a larger number of levels will also decrease the number of subjects per level and hence threaten the (cross-sample) stability of the bias analysis. As a rule of thumb, we do not advise using score levels with less than 50 persons. In empirical applications it is not uncommon to find that the score widths of the groups were chosen in such a way that the number of subjects in the groups are made as similar as possible (e.g., 10 score groups of approximately 50 persons each). If there is uncertainty about the number of levels to be used, an exploratory strategy can be adopted in which the number is varied in a series of analyses. Quite likely, items that show substantial bias will be found independent of the number of levels distinguished; findings will probably show more inconsistency across score levels for less biased items.

When score levels have to be concatenated, a score distribution for the combined samples can be composed to identify cutoff points for forming appropriately equal-sized groups in each culture. An example of a hypothetical data matrix and SPSS instructions required to produce such a distribution and to carry out the conditional analysis of variance is given in Box 4.3. When score distributions of cultural groups show

BOX 4.2
Schematic Overview of
Item Bias Detection Techniques

A taxonomy is presented here that is based on three dichotomous categorizations that are relevant to the user of the techniques (see Table 4.2). First, a distinction is made between models that are based on either linear or nonlinear model equations. Linear models such as analysis of variance tend to be applied to interval- or ratio-level data, whereas nominal data are more frequently analyzed with nonlinear models (such as item response and log-linear models).

Second, if the aim is to arrive at statistically adequate tests of item bias, it is important to choose a bias statistic with a known sampling distribution. All bias statistics give some evaluation of the discrepancy of score patterns across groups but not all of them allow for a statistical test of its significance, because their sampling distributions are unknown. Item response theory is mentioned in Table 4.2 as having both unknown and known sampling distributions. In former days, several statistics were proposed that did not have a known sampling distribution, such as measures of the areas between item characteristic curves (e.g., Shepard, Camilli, & Averill, 1981). Item bias statistics based on item response theory that were more recently proposed usually have a known sampling distribution. Thus, Lord (1980) has developed a procedure that is based on a two-parameter item response model. The procedure has been applied by, among others, Raju, Drasgow, and Slinde (1993). Other procedures with known sampling distributions are given by Thissen, Steinberg, and Wainer (1993). Andersen (1973) has developed a fit test for a one-parameter model that can be easily extended for detecting item bias; applications of this procedure can be found in Tanzer, Gittler, and Sim (1994) and Tanzer, Gittler, and Ellis (1995).

Third, a distinction is made between conditional and unconditional procedures. In conditional procedures the sample is split up into score-level groups;

considerable overlap, it may not be difficult to find cutoff points. With highly dissimilar score distributions it may be necessary to lump many scores together, thereby unavoidably decreasing the power to detect item bias.

TABLE 4.2 Schematic Overview of Differential Item Functioning
Techniques (adapted from van de Vijver, 1994)

	Model Equation	
Sampling Distribution	*Linear*	*Nonlinear*
Unconditional procedures		
Unknown	Item-total correlations	Delta plots (Angoff, 1982)
Known	Analysis of variance (Cleary & Hilton, 1968)	—
Conditional Procedures		
Unknown	—	Item response theory (Shepard, Camilli, & Averill, 1981)
Known	Standardized p-difference (Dorans & Kulick, 1986); analysis of variance with score level as one of the independent variables (Box 4.3)	Item response theory (Lord, 1980; Thissen, Steinberg, & Wainer, 1993); Mantel-Haenszel procedure (Holland & Thayer, 1988)

unconditional procedures compute bias statistics for the whole sample without such a split in score groups. Lord (1980) has shown that unconditional statistics can yield misleading results by failing to identify biased items, especially when the score distributions obtained in various cultural groups are widely different. A simple visual inspection of item averages can lead to incorrect conclusions (this is known as Simpson's paradox; see Dorans & Holland, 1993, pp. 37-38). Unconditional procedures are nonetheless presented here in the table because of their widespread use in the past. Furthermore, many unconditional procedures can be easily made conditional by adding score group as an additional variable in the design, as illustrated in the conditional analysis of variance discussed in Box 4.3.

After having determined the cutoff points to define score levels, the analysis of variance in which bias will be scrutinized can be carried out. The significance of three effects is tested in the analysis. The first is the significance of score level. This is seldom of any interest; the corresponding F ratio indicates whether the differences in average scores

BOX 4.3
Item Bias Detection Using Analysis of Variance

1. Sample of data matrix

Subject	Culture	Item01	Item02	...	Item 20
1	1	3	4	...	2
2	1	2	5	...	4
.	.	.	.	...	.
.	.	.	.	...	.
.	.	.	.	...	.
500	1	2	2	...	3
1	2	4	5	...	2
.	.	.	.	...	.
.	.	.	.	...	.
.	.	.	.	...	.
500	2	4	2	...	3

2. Instructions to compute total test scores

```
COMPUTE sum = SUM(item01 to item20) .
EXECUTE .
```

3. Instruction to find cutoff points

```
FREQUENCIES    VARIABLES=sum    /NTILES= 8.
```

Comment: The NTILES parameter specifies the number of score groups.

across score levels are significant. They usually are, indicating that individuals at lower score levels have lower scores on the item than persons at higher score levels. The two remaining effects are more relevant. When both the main effect of culture and the interaction of level and culture are nonsignificant, the item is taken to be unbiased. An example of such an item is given in Figure 4.1 (panel a). The

4. Instructions to define score levels

```
RECODE
sum
(20 thru 32 = 1) (33 thru 39 = 2) (40 thru 45 = 3)
(46 thru 49 = 4) (50 thru 53 = 5) (54 thru 58 = 6)
(59 thru 67 = 7) (68 thru 100 = 8) INTO level .
EXECUTE .
```

Comment: Cutoff points are usually determined on the basis of a prior analysis of the grouped frequency distribution of the scores in the combined cultural groups.

5. Instructions to carry out a conditional analysis of variance

```
ANOVA VARIABLES = item01 BY culture(1 2) level(1 8)
/MAXORDERS ALL /METHOD UNIQUE /FORMAT LABELS .
```

6. Output (edited)

Source of Variation	Sum of Squares	DF	Mean Square	F	Sig of F
Main Effects					
CULTURE	**3.489**	**1**	**3.489**	**4.648**	**.031**
LEVEL	117.505	7	16.786	22.368	.00
2-Way Interactions					
CULTURE LEVEL	**7.417**	**7**	**1.060**	**1.412**	**.197**
Residual	738.459	984	.750		
Total	875.741	999	.877		

Comment: The most important effects are printed in bold. The main effect of culture is significant ($p = .031$), which indicates the presence of uniform bias. There is no nonuniform bias because the interaction component is not significant ($p = .197$).

horizontal axis represents the score levels (note that the same score levels apply to both groups). The vertical axis presents the mean of the first group minus the mean of the second group for each score level. Unbiased items will have curves that do not differ from zero in any systematic way. In the case of item bias, the departure from zero will be systematic. Individuals from one cultural group may have higher scores on an item than individuals from another cultural group even when they have the same total test score. Mellenbergh (1982) has called this uniform bias (see Figure 4.1, panel b; see also Chapter 2, Implications of Bias for Equivalence). A significant main effect of culture means that the curve of Figure 4.1 is consistently above or below zero. As a hypothetical example, suppose that a test of world geography is administered to 500 youngsters in Poland and 500 youngsters in Japan and that one of the items is *What is the capital of Germany?* This item can be expected to be easier for Polish than for Japanese youngsters irrespective of their overall geographical knowledge.

The last effect of interest in the analysis of variance is the interaction of score level and culture. A significant interaction indicates that the difference between cultural groups is not invariant across score levels. The item discriminates better in one group than in the other. This has been labeled nonuniform bias (Mellenbergh, 1982). An example is given in Figure 4.1 (panel c). Again, the curve connecting the cross-cultural differences in average scores departs systematically from zero; however, the departure is not uniform across score levels in this case. As a hypothetical example, suppose that German and Zimbabwean parents are asked to rate their children on a set of intelligence-related characteristics and that one of the items is obedience. Let us assume that obedience is more related to the child's intelligence for the Zimbabwean parents. The item will then show a better discrimination across score levels among these parents. It may be noted that in empirical applications, nonuniform bias has been much less frequently reported than uniform bias.

Item Bias Detection in Dichotomous Scores: The Mantel-Haenszel Statistic

The Mantel-Haenszel procedure is conceptually related to the conditional analysis of variance just described. The major difference involves the type of data analyzed: Whereas interval- or ratio-level data are needed for an analysis of variance, the Mantel-Haenszel procedure analyzes dichotomous data. The computation of the statistic is illustrated in Box 4.4.

The properties of the currently highly popular Mantel-Haenszel procedure have been thoroughly studied. The statistic has been found to be powerful in identifying biased items, provided the number of

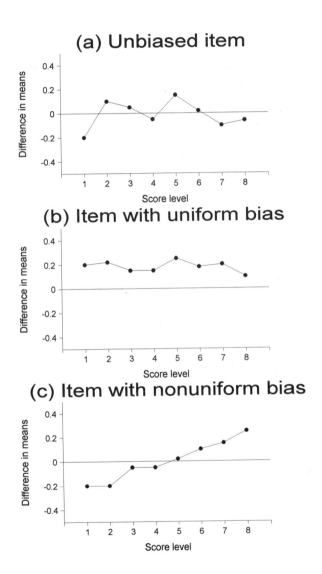

Figure 4.1. Hypothetical Examples of (a) an Unbiased Item, (b) an Item With Uniform Bias, and (c) an Item With Nonuniform Bias

---

BOX 4.4
Item Bias Detection Using
the Mantel-Haenszel Statistic

The computation of the Mantel-Haenszel statistic starts with a split of the sample into score levels. In the analysis of variance we work with item scores; in the present case, item scores are combined into frequency tables. Per item, a set of frequency tables can be derived, one for each score level. For a particular score level, such a table is presented as follows (m refers to the score group):

Group	Item score = 0	Item score = 1	Total
Culture A	N_{Am0}	N_{Am1}	$N_{Am.}$
Culture B	N_{Bm0}	N_{Bm1}	$N_{Bm.}$
Total	$N_{.m0}$	$N_{.m1}$	$N_{.m.}$

For each item there are m of these 2 × 2 tables. The Mantel-Haenszel procedure tests whether the odds of having a score of 1 for an item is identical in both cultures for all m score levels. The test statistic is defined as

$$[\sum_m | N_{Bm1} - \sum_m E(N_{Bm1}) | - .5)]^2 / \sum_m Var(N_{Bm1}),$$

in which

$$E(N_{Bm1}) = N_{.m1} N_{Bm.} / N_{.m.} \text{ and}$$
$$Var\,(N_{Bm1}) = N_{Am.}\, N_{Bm.}\, N_{.m0}\, N_{.m1} / [\, N_{.m.}^2\, (N_{.m.} - 1)\,].$$

The statistic follows a χ^2 distribution with one degree of freedom. Items with values higher than a critical value (3.84 for $\alpha = .05$ and 6.63 for $\alpha = .01$) are taken to be biased.

score groups used is sufficiently large (e.g., Clauser et al., 1994). Fischer (1993) has shown that the Mantel-Haenszel procedure and the Rasch model, a popular model in item response theory (see Box 4.6 below), are closely related. The Mantel-Haenszel procedure tests whether a Rasch model with the same item parameter holds for the two groups studied.

The Mantel-Haenszel is available in statistical packages such as SPSS and SAS (though data manipulation is usually required to transform the data into an appropriate form). As an alternative, specialized computer programs have become available recently (e.g., Nandakumar, 1993; Rogers & Hambleton, 1994).

From a practical perspective, the Mantel-Haenszel procedure shows two shortcomings. First, it allows for pairwise comparisons only. Data sets involving more than two cultural groups have to be split in the analyses. Such a split can have undesirable consequences. If an instrument has been administered in 10 countries, then 45 pairwise comparisons can be made and it is difficult to integrate the results into an overall picture. The problem is avoided if one group can be defined as the reference group. When an instrument has been translated from one source language into several target languages, the data obtained with the source version can be defined as the reference set to which all other data are compared. In this case, the question addressed is the accuracy of the translation and not the delineation of a universal set of unbiased items.

A second problem of the Mantel-Haenszel procedure is related to the distinction between uniform and nonuniform bias. The procedure can adequately detect uniform bias, but its power to detect nonuniform bias is low. In order to alleviate the problem, Mazor, Clauser, and Hambleton (1994) proposed splitting the sample into low and high scorers and carrying out a bias analysis on these two groups separately. The authors reported that this procedure led to increased power in detecting nonuniform bias.

Both problems can be solved by using log-linear models (Van der Flier, Mellenbergh, Adèr, & Wijn, 1984). These models analyze contingency tables of two or more cultural groups in terms of main effects and interactions in the same way as an analysis of variance; log-linear analysis can be seen as the counterpart of analysis of variance for nominal-level data. The data for a bias analysis using a log-linear model are set up in the same way as in the Mantel-Haenszel procedure. Both uniform and nonuniform bias can be detected. A significant main effect of culture points to uniform bias, and a significant interaction between culture and score level indicates nonuniform bias. An example of the setup of the data matrix, the SPSS instructions, and the output is given in Box 4.5.

BOX 4.5
Item Bias Detection Using Log-Linear Modeling

1. Sample of data matrix

culture	item	itemscor	level	freq
1	1	0	1	20
2	1	0	1	50
1	1	0	2	35
2	1	0	2	70

Explanation of symbols:

- Culture: Cultural group (number of levels is the number of cultures involved);
- Item: Item of the instrument;
- Itemscor: Item score (2 levels: 0 and 1);
- Level: Score level (number of levels will vary, depending on the number of levels distinguished);
- Freq: Number of persons in that category (e.g., there are 20 persons in the first score group of Culture 1 with a score of 0 on the first item).

2. Instructions for the log-linear analysis

```
WEIGHT BY freq.
BREAK BY ITEM.
```

Item Bias Detection Using Item Response Theory

Item response theory (IRT) represents a more general approach to the assessment of differential item functioning (e.g., Hambleton & Swaminathan, 1985; Hulin, 1987). Because most current work on IRT involves dichotomous variables, only this case is discussed. Readers who are interested in IRT models for polychotomous variables are referred to Samejima (1969). A brief introduction to IRT models is given in Box 4.6.

```
LOGLINEAR
    itemscor(0,1) by culture(0 1) level(1 10)
    /PRINT= FREQ RESID
    /CRITERIA ITERATION(20) CONVERGE(.001) DELTA(.5)
    /design itemscor itemscor by level
    /design itemscor itemscor by level itemscor by culture.
```

Comment: The BREAK command is used to analyze the data for all items in a single set of commands; the first DESIGN command tests the absence of bias, the second the presence of uniform and nonuniform bias.

- Test of first model:

```
Model specification: itemscor itemscor BY level
Goodness-of-Fit test statistics
Likelihood Ratio Chi Square = 38.21855  DF = 10  P = .000
            Pearson Chi Square = 38.28858  DF = 10  P = .000
```

Conclusion: A model without score level and cultural group has a poor fit; so, the item is biased.

- Test of second model:

```
Model specification: itemscor itemscor BY level
    itemscor BY culture.
Goodness-of-Fit test statistics
Likelihood Ratio Chi Square = 21.32219  DF = 9  P = .011
            Pearson Chi Square = 21.32685  DF = 9  P = .011
```

Conclusion: The inclusion of culture leads to a significant improvement in fit ($\chi^2 = 38.22 - 21.32$, $df = 10 - 9$); the item shows uniform bias. The model still shows a poor fit, however, pointing to nonuniform bias.

Prior to an IRT analysis, preliminary analyses have to be carried out. IRT assumes that a scale is unidimensional, and the unidimensionality of the scale must be established. If the scale is multidimensional, each unidimensional subscale should be examined separately. The easiest way to check the dimensionality of a scale may seem to be to examine its alpha coefficient. However, alpha coefficients are not sensitive to detecting the multidimensionality of a scale. Factor analysis is more appropriate, and two approaches have been frequently employed. First,

BOX 4.6
Item Response Theory

IRT proposes that item responses can be related to a latent trait by means of a logistic curve, usually specified by three parameters. The probability of a positive response to an item is defined as a function of an individual's standing on the latent trait that the item assesses. The function has three parameters for each item. A graph plotting these probabilities against the latent trait is called an item characteristic curve (ICC); it takes the form of an S-shaped curve. In an ICC, the y axis usually represents the probability of giving a positive response, which ranges from 0 to 1. The x axis represents the latent trait, which is usually standardized with a mean equal to 0 and a standard deviation equal to 1. For the purpose of the presentation, the range of the latent trait is usually set at –3.5 to +3.5 in plotting an ICC. The probability of a positive response is defined as:

$$P_i(\theta) = c_i + (1 - c_i) \frac{\exp[Da_i(\theta - b_i)]}{1 + \exp[Da_i(\theta - b_i)]},$$

where θ refers to the standing of an individual on a latent trait, which may be a specific ability, belief, value, or attitude. $P_i(\theta)$ refers to the probability of a positive response to item i given that the standing of an individual on the latent trait is θ. D is a constant that is usually set at 1 or 1.7 (in which case the ICC is almost identical to a curve for a normal ogive model). The item discrimination parameter, a, expresses the discrimination capability of the item. It is proportional to the slope ("steepness") of the ICC at the inflection point (at which the slope of the ICC is maximal). Larger values of a are associated with steeper ICCs, which indicate higher levels of discrimination. The item difficulty parameter, b, determines the difficulty level of the item and is represented by the value on the horizontal axis at the inflection point. Larger values of b are associated with items that are more difficult and require a higher level on the latent trait for a positive response. The b parameter is concerned with the relative position of the ICC along the horizontal axis. ICCs with larger values of b tend to be located to the right of the midpoint of the horizontal axis (which is 0). The pseudo-chance level parameter, c, expresses the extent to which guessing is involved in responding to the item. The c parameter is the lower asymptote of an ICC, and it represents the probability of giving a positive response (or endorsing the item) by the respondents with a low standing on the latent trait. For items with larger values of c, respondents with lower levels of the latent trait have a relatively higher probability of giving a

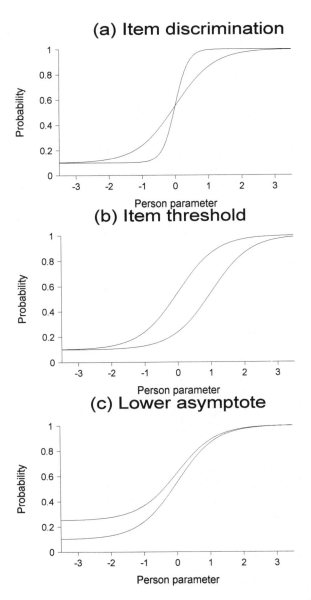

Figure 4.2. Hypothetical Item Characteristic Curves of Items That Differ Only in (a) the Item Discrimination Parameter, (b) the Item Difficulty Parameter, and (c) the Lower Asymptote

BOX 4.6 Continued

positive response. See Figure 4.2 for ICCs with different values of the three parameters. The meaning of the a parameter is illustrated by panel a. As the value of a increases, the ICC becomes steeper. The meaning of the b parameter is illustrated by panel b. As the value of b increases, the ICC shifts to the right. The meaning of the c parameter is illustrated by panel c. As the value of c increases, the value of the lower asymptote increases and the ICC will move upward.

The Rasch model is a special IRT model (Molenaar & Fischer, 1995). It assumes that there is no (pseudo-)guessing (i.e., $c = 0$) and that all items have the same value of the discrimination parameter value of 1. Only the item threshold parameter, b, is retained and allowed to vary across items. The normalization constant is usually fixed at 1. The probability of a correct answer is given by

$$P_i(\theta) = \frac{\exp(\theta - b_i)}{1 + \exp(\theta - b_i)}.$$

IRT is applicable to ability tests as well as to instruments measuring other constructs such as attitudes and beliefs on a Likert-type scale. When the latent trait is concerned with ability, the pseudo-chance level parameter is meaningful and necessary. When respondents encounter items that they do not know how to answer in an ability test, they may try to guess the correct answer. The c parameter is an attempt to reflect the effect of guessing on their scores. For other constructs, such as attitudes and personality traits, guessing or random responses are unlikely, and two-parameter models, which exclude the pseudo-chance level parameter, are often employed. When the sample is not large enough to estimate the c parameter adequately, the parameter is often fixed at some value; in multiple choice testing the value is often set at 1 divided by the number of alternatives (the probability of a correct answer with random guessing).

Lord (1980) suggested that a principal components factor analysis can be conducted, with the largest off-diagonal correlations as the communality estimates. The eigenvalues of the matrix are then calculated, and if the first eigenvalue is substantially larger than the second eigenvalue, unidimensionality can be assumed.

Second, Drasgow and Lissak (1983) have proposed a more sophisticated procedure, modified parallel analysis (MPA), for detecting the multidimensionality of a scale. Current applications of IRT are mostly based on dichotomous variables, and tetrachoric correlations need to be used. Factor analysis based on tetrachoric correlations may yield too many factors (Hambleton & Swaminathan, 1985). In Drasgow and Lissak's (1983) procedure, the eigenvalues of the data set are estimated as in the first approach. In addition, a synthetic data set is created, with item and ability parameters estimated from the real data. These estimated parameters and a random number generator are used to produce a data set that is truly unidimensional. This synthetic data set is factor analyzed in the same way as the real data set, and the eigenvalues derived from the two data sets are compared. Multidimensionality is indicated if the second eigenvalue of the real data set is substantially larger than the second eigenvalue of the synthetic data set (see Hambleton, Swaminathan, & Rogers, 1991, and Hattie, 1985, for several other methods for evaluating the unidimensionality of a scale).

An item is biased in IRT if one or more of its parameters differ significantly across cultural groups (Hambleton & Swaminathan, 1985, chap. 13). Differences in the item difficulty parameter point to uniform bias (panel b of Figure 4.2), whereas differences in the discrimination parameter indicate nonuniform bias (panel a).

Two approaches are currently popular in detecting item bias using IRT models, namely, parameter- and model-based comparisons; both are illustrated in Box 4.6. The parameter-based approach is based on a comparison of the parameters of the IRT models across cultural groups. This is the dominant approach in cross-cultural research and has been used to study cultural differences in self-concept (Leung & Drasgow, 1986), job satisfaction (Candell & Hulin, 1986), intelligence (Ellis, 1990), and attitudes toward mental health (Ellis & Kimmel, 1992).

The standard procedure for the application of the parameter-based approach for detecting item bias across cultures is as follows:

1. An item response theory model with the appropriate number of parameters is selected to fit the data in each culture. The two-parameter model is used for attitudinal data and personality measures.
2. The parameters identified for each cultural group are equated on the same metric through an iterative linking procedure (Stocking & Lord, 1983).

3. Biased items are detected and eliminated with the aid of item characteristic curves and a chi-square test (Lord, 1980). The parameters are
   equated again with the linking procedure applied to unbiased items only;
   this procedure stops when no biased items are detected.
4. The biased items identified are eliminated from the scale before cross-
   cultural comparisons are made.

In the model-comparison approach, two models, the compact model
and the augmented model, are compared to determine whether there is
item bias (Thissen, Steinberg, & Wainer, 1993). To illustrate this procedure, consider a case in which there are two groups, the focal group and
the reference group. The compact model assumes that there is no
difference between the item parameters for all the items across the two
groups. A chi-square statistic can be obtained, which reflects the goodness of fit of the compact model to the data. The augmented model is
set up by assuming that the parameters of the item that is tested for bias
are different in the two groups. Another chi-square statistic is then
obtained for the augmented model. These two chi-square statistics are
compared, and if the difference is significant, it is concluded that the
item studied shows item bias. The compact model is hierarchically
nested within the augmented model, which enables a likelihood ratio
test. If the chi-square statistics of the two models do not differ significantly from each other, it can be concluded that the two models are
similar and that the item is unbiased. For an illustration of how to
conduct this analysis, see Thissen et al. (1993) and Box 4.7. Holland and
Wainer (1993) regard the model-comparison approach as superior to the
parameter-based approach.

IRT has a number of features that make it desirable for cross-cultural
research. First, the estimates of item parameters do not depend on the
standing of a group on the latent trait studied. This is contrary to
classical test theory, in which the difficulty of an item, operationalized
as the item average, depends on the average ability level of the group.
Analogously, the estimation of a person's standing on a latent trait in
IRT is independent of the items used. An interesting implication of this
property of IRT models is that using identical stimulus sets is no longer
required when comparing different cultural groups. Provided that the
common set of items is not too small and still represents the construct
fairly well, IRT models overcome the problem of most level-oriented

---

BOX 4.7
Item Bias Detection
Using Item Response Theory

The example is based on a study by Huang, Church, and Katigbak (1995). These authors administered the NEO Personality Inventory, a measure of the big-five personality model, to 432 Filipino and 610 American college students. Prior to the analyses, the data were transformed from the original 5-point scale to dichotomous scores. Item bias in the Agreeableness Scale was explored with a three-parameter IRT model.

Model-Based Comparison

Data were analyzed using the BILOG program (Mislevy & Bock, 1990). The BILOG input is as follows:

```
GLOBAL DFN='MYFILE.DAT', NPARM=3, NTE=2;
```

Comment: This line specifies the raw data file (DFN), the number of item parameters (NPARM), and the number of subtests (NTE). The American and Filipino items are analyzed jointly, except for the item to be studied for bias. This item was analyzed separately for both groups, thereby increasing the test length from 18 to 19 items.

```
LENGTH NITE=(18,19);
```

Comment: This line specifies the number of items in the subtests.

```
INPUT NTOT=54, NALT=5, NID=4; (4A1,5X,54A1)
```

Comment: The line specifies the total number of items in the original data records (NTOT), the number of response alternatives (NALT), and the number of fields for respondents' identification. The end of the line gives the format statement to read the data.

```
TEST1 TNA=AGREE, ITEMS=(1,2,3,4,5,6,7,8,9,10,11,12,13,14,15,
16,17,18);
```

Comment: The line specifies a name and the item numbers for the first test.

```
TEST2 TNA=ITEM3, ITEMS=(1,2,4,5,6,7,8,9,10,11,12,13,14,15,
16,17,18,21,39);
```

(continued)

BOX 4.7 Continued

Comment: The line specifies the item numbers for the second test. This is a test of bias in the third item. The data are organized in such a way in the file that the first 18 responses are coded for both U.S. and Filipino respondents, the next 18 for the U.S. respondents, and the last 18 for the Filipino respondents (items number 21 and 39 refer to the third item in the U.S. and Filipino groups, respectively).

```
CALIB TPRIOR, SPRIOR, GPRIOR, READPRI, CHI=18, IDI=0;
```

Comment: The line specifies that prior distributions on the threshold, slope, and lower asymptote are used (TPRIOR, SPRIOR, GPRIOR), that priors of the lower asymptote are specified below (READPRI), that the minimum number of items for the computation of the chi-square item fit statistics is 18, and that the standard normal distribution is the prior person parameter distribution.

```
PRIORS1 ALPHA=(45 <values omitted here> 51),
        BETA=(157 <values omitted here> 163);
PRIORS2 ALPHA=(45 <values omitted here> 43),
        BETA=(157 <values omitted here> 159);
```

Comment: The lines specify the priors of the lower asymptote.

```
SCORE   METHOD=2, RSC=2, LOC=0.0, SCA=1.0;
```

Comment: The line specifies the method of estimating scale scores that is (Bayesian) expected a posteriori (METHOD=2), the type of rescaling required (RSC=2 means that the scale is determined from the 17 common items), the location constant for rescaling (LOC), and the scale constant for rescaling (SCA). In the study of item bias the slope and threshold parameters are free in both cultural groups, whereas the lower asymptote is fixed.

The most important parts of the output are as follows:

The log likelihood for the compact model:

```
-2 LOG LIKELIHOOD =      19403.8411
```

The log likelihood for the augmented model:

```
-2 LOG LIKELIHOOD =      19353.9192
```

Comment: the difference between the likelihoods (i.e., 19403.8411 − 19353.9192) is distributed as a chi-square variable with 2 degrees of freedom (because two more parameters were estimated in the latter analysis). The difference is highly significant; it is concluded that the item is biased.

Parameter Equating Method

The method is illustrated using the input and output of Kim and Cohen's (1991) IRTDIF program.

Input specifications:

```
AGREEABLENESS SCALE
3-PARAMETER MODEL WITH FIXED C
SCALING CONSTANT D: 1.000
NUMBER OF ITEM IS:      18
1ST FILE NAME IS:
USAGREE.COV
RECORD SKIPPED FROM 1ST FILE:    2
1ST FILE FORMAT IS:
(12X,5F12.6/12X,F12.6//)
2ND FILE NAME IS:
PHAGREE.COV
RECORD SKIPPED FROM 2ND FILE:    2
2ND FILE FORMAT IS:
(12X,5F12.6/12X,F12.6//)
EQUATING SLOPE A     :    1.000000
EQUATING INTERCEPT K:    0.000000
CLOSED-INTERVAL THETA1 IS:   -4.000000
CLOSED-INTERVAL THETA2 IS:    4.000000
OUTPUT FILE NAME IS:
AGREEABL.DIF
```

The output is as follows:

ITEM	CHI-SQUARE	P-VALUE	
1	3.434513	0.179558	
2	9.076082	0.010694	*
3	36.267563	0.000000	***
4	39.664066	0.000000	***
5	6.731154	0.034542	*

(continued)

BOX 4.7 Continued

6	10.447322	0.005388 **
7	1.500858	0.472164
8	2.033991	0.361680
9	10.202586	0.006089 **
10	6.316631	0.042497 *
11	12.778557	0.001679 **
12	20.007557	0.000045 ***
13	18.921215	0.000078 ***
14	3.295309	0.192501
15	1.783963	0.409843
16	12.471228	0.001958 **
17	1.552431	0.460144
18	0.576895	0.749426

Comment: The results of Lord's (1980) chi-square procedure are reproduced. The output for all 18 items is reported. A small p value points to item bias. Note that the third item is also identified as biased in this analysis.

techniques that only fully identical instruments can be used in cross-cultural comparisons.

Second, fit tests can be conducted to evaluate the extent to which empirical data conform to the theoretical model (e.g., Hambleton & Swaminathan, 1985; Lord, 1980; Van den Wollenberg, 1988). It should be pointed out that if a substantial proportion of the items tested are found to be biased, the validity of the instrument is suspect. An expedient approach would then be to refrain from cross-cultural comparisons; additional research may be required to identify sources of bias.

The most important limitations of IRT are twofold. First, the applicability of item response models may be reduced by the strict assumptions that have to be met, particularly in the case of the Rasch model (in this model an item is characterized by only one parameter, namely its difficulty/popularity). Moreover, responses in all cultural groups are assumed to be generated independently; no transfer between item responses is allowed, such as loss of motivation, fatigue, or learning from previous items. Second, large sample sizes are required to obtain stable estimates, particularly in the three-parameter model.

How Can We Deal With Item Bias?

There are various ways to deal with bias (see also Poortinga & Van der Flier, 1988). First, bias can be seen as an indicator that an instrument is inadequate for cross-cultural comparison; as a consequence, a researcher can decide to refrain from such comparisons. Such an approach is prudent though restrictive because item bias is likely to occur in any study of highly dissimilar cultural groups. The approach shows a sharp contrast with the common practice of carrying out cross-cultural comparisons without an analysis of item bias (or any other type of bias, for that matter) and of interpreting observed cross-cultural differences at face value.

Alternatively, item bias can be seen as providing important clues about cross-cultural differences. Unbiased items define culture-common aspects of a construct and biased items denote cultural idiosyncrasies. A comprehensive picture is then developed based on universal and culture-specific elements of a construct. The fruitfulness of the approach largely depends on the success of finding reasons for the presence and absence of bias that can be integrated into such a picture.

Finally, the most common way to deal with item bias is to treat it as a disturbance at the item level that has to be removed. Only unbiased items constitute a solid basis for cross-cultural comparison, and an item bias analysis aims at identifying and removing the presumably biased items.

Such a procedure can be applied in an iterative and a noniterative way. In the latter case a single run is carried out to identify item bias; this amounts to a single analysis in the case of IRT and to an analysis per item in the case of the Mantel-Haenszel procedure or analysis of variance. The iterative procedure analyzes all data in a single run (in the same way as the noniterative procedure) and identifies the most biased item (the item with the largest uniform and/or nonuniform bias). If the bias is statistically significant, the item is eliminated. This reduces the instrument by one item. The analysis is then repeated without the biased item. The procedure is straightforward though tedious, particularly in the case of an analysis of variance. After an item has been eliminated, new score levels and cutoff points have to be determined before the analyses of variance for the remaining items can be carried out. The steps are repeated until no more items show a significant bias.

Iterative and noniterative procedures do not always show the same results. The choice between them can sometimes be based on theoretical grounds. The mathematical accuracy of the noniterative procedure has been shown for the Mantel-Haenszel procedure and item bias statistics based on the Rasch model (Lewis, 1993). There are also practical considerations, however. Because iterative procedures redefine score levels in each iteration, they allow for finer shifts of the standard for evaluating bias. During the bias analyses the total score on the instrument may take on a slightly different meaning due to the elimination of particular sets of items. As a hypothetical example, suppose that an instrument of 20 items has a subset of 5 biased items on the same topic; the total score will have a different meaning when these 5 items are removed.

Removal of item bias can have different outcomes on the size of observed cross-cultural differences. Burton and Burton (1993) found that the deletion of biased items in performance tests administered to various cultural groups in the United States left the size of cross-cultural differences unaffected, whereas Ellis (1990) found that statistical tests of cross-cultural differences on subtests of an intelligence test administered to American and German students revealed dissimilar patterns of significance before and after bias removal.

Item Bias: Conclusions

The practical value of item bias checks should not be underestimated. Item bias statistics are valuable tools in tracing such item anomalies as poor translations and inadequate word choice. Item bias statistics should be routinely reported in cross-cultural studies. There is no rationale for the common practice of taking observed cross-cultural differences at face value without a check of item accuracy. Furthermore, it is important to explore reasons for item bias. A search for common aspects of biased items can be recommended, possibly aided by one or more local experts. For instance, Ellis et al. (1993) studied possible translation errors in a personality questionnaire that was translated from German into English by presenting items that were found to be biased to a group of bilinguals.

Some work in the item bias tradition seems to assume that the removal of item bias will lead to scalar equivalence and to bias-free comparisons. We do not agree with the implied reduction of bias to item bias; construct and method bias may not be identified by item bias techniques. This problem is especially serious when score distributions from different cultures show little overlap, and construct and method bias should also be examined; item bias may create relatively mild distortions compared to the influence of the other types of bias. Moreover, when the score distributions are highly dissimilar, the accuracy of the assumption that persons from different cultural groups with equal test scores have an equal standing on the latent trait can become questionable. For example, suppose that the Raven's Progressive Matrices is administered to a random sample of adults in Tokyo and to illiterate Bushmen. It would be naive to assume that Japanese and Bushmen with the same total score are equally intelligent.

What conclusions can be drawn from item bias studies? Do these conclusions have implications for proper design and analysis of cross-cultural research? A first conclusion of item bias studies is that it is often difficult to identify reasons why an item is biased. Second, results of different procedures for identifying bias often do not show the same results. Convergence of bias statistics has been studied from several perspectives. First, some studies have addressed the convergence of findings across widely different statistical techniques. Low to moderate correlations between different methods have been repeatedly reported (e.g., Devine & Raju, 1982; Ironson & Subkoviak, 1979; Reise, Widaman, & Pugh, 1993; Rudner, Getson, & Knight, 1980; Shepard et al., 1981). Stronger correlations have been reported by Rogers and Swaminathan (1993) and Raju, Drasgow, and Slinde (1993).

Second, the stability of item bias statistics has been found to be poor, both in test-retest studies and in cross-validations. Skaggs and Lissitz (1992) studied the stability of item bias indices, among them the Mantel-Haenszel statistic, in items from a curriculum-based mathematics test across different administrations of the same items. The stability of the bias indices was "modest at best" (p. 227). Hoover and Kolen (1984), studying the Iowa Tests of Basic Skills (an achievement test), reported a low stability of bias statistics across randomly chosen samples of Blacks and Whites in the United States. Ellis et al. (1993) found more agreement in a cross-validation of item bias in a personality questionnaire.

Third, the correspondence of judgmental and statistical methods has been examined, addressing the question of the extent to which experts and statistical procedures agree on the occurrence of item bias. Data on a mathematical test from more than 3,000 schoolchildren in the fourth through eighth grades were analyzed for bias, and three experts made subjective judgments about item bias. There was little agreement between statistical and subjective methods (Plake, 1980). Huang, Church, and Katigbak (1995) analyzed the responses of Filipino and American college students to the NEO Personality Inventory, a measure of the big-five factor personality model. The authors found that subjective judgments by bilingual experts as to which items would show item bias were not in agreement with statistical methods. Low correlations between judgmental and statistical methods have also been reported by Engelhard, Hansche, and Rutledge (1990).

The reasons for the lack of convergence are varied. First, several item bias studies have reported small effects. Such effects, even though significant, are by definition hard to cross-validate. Several studies in the United States, usually comparing Whites with either Blacks or Hispanics, have shown that differences in item averages for matched groups are seldom substantial; the difference in proportion of correct responses on mental tests between matched Blacks and Whites is usually not larger than .10. The small effect sizes observed are to some extent a consequence of the samples in bias studies. Most studies include different cultural groups in the United States. Comparisons of groups with larger cultural distances may well reveal more items to be biased. For instance, Nenty and Dinero (1981), comparing Nigerian high school students and American university students on the Cattell Culture Fair Intelligence Test, found more than half of the items to be biased. Van der Flier (1982) found a high percentage of items to be biased in a study of exclusion and verbal analogy tests among Kenyan and English schoolchildren. Both studies reported considerably more items to be biased than the 10% that is commonly found in research among ethnic groups in the United States.

Another reason for the lack of convergence is the heterogeneity of statistical models used. All popular statistical techniques have been applied for detecting item bias. It is hardly surprising that these techniques do not always show identical results. Furthermore, unconditional and conditional methods for detecting item bias can produce dissimilar results. Unconditional methods will often confound valid differences and item bias. A convergence of findings regarding uniform bias is more likely for currently popular techniques such as the Mantel-Haenszel procedure, item response models, and log-linear models. All these models are different "translations" of the same definition of bias, and all compare performance levels across total score levels.

Interaction effects in analyses of variance are infamous for their cross-sample instability. An example can be found in research on aptitude-treatment interactions in educational psychology (Cronbach & Snow, 1977). An example from the cross-cultural literature can be found in Amir and Sharon's (1987) replication of common Western paradigms from experimental social psychology in Israel. The authors found some replicability of main effects but a notorious instability of interaction effects. The same instability may beleaguer nonuniform item bias, which also involves an interaction component.

Given the poor knowledge as to what kind of items can be expected to be biased, it is not surprising that bias studies have not generated new insights on recommendable practices in instrument construction for cross-cultural research. Rather, recommendations offered by item bias researchers are of a general nature. For example, on the basis of a comparison of the performance on educational tests of migrant (Turkish and Moroccan) and native Dutch pupils, Kok (1988) suggests using short sentences and avoiding uncommon words wherever possible. Schmitt, Holland, and Dorans (1993) stress the influence of the first language when the instrument is administered in the second language; both positive and negative transfer can occur. For example, item bias is more likely to occur in a comparison of Hispanics and Anglo-Saxon Americans when Spanish and English words have a common root but a different meaning. The authors mention the example of *enviable*, which means *sendable* in Spanish. O'Neill and McPeek (1993) point to consistent differences in the performance of Blacks and Whites in the United States on analogy items. Blacks tend to score higher than Whites (matched on test score) on analogies about human relations (e.g., *reprimand : reprove :: eulogy : praise*) and Whites higher than matched Blacks on science content (e.g., *bark : tree :: skin : fruit*). Scheuneman (1987) studied bias in items for American Blacks and Whites on the Graduate Record Examination General Test. Various hypotheses about the influence of formal characteristics on item bias were tested (such as a negative phrasing of item stem, clarity of content, and ordinal position of the correct alternative). Some systematic relationships were found; yet "what emerges most clearly from the study is how little we know about the mechanisms that produce differential performance between black and white examinees" (p. 117).

In sum, the overall picture is gloomy; as Bond (1993) put it: "Theories about why items behave differently across groups can be described only as primitive" (p. 278); or in Linn's (1993) words: "The majority of items with large *dif* values seem to defy explanation of the kind that can lead to more general principles of sound test development practice" (p. 359). The only item characteristic that shows a fairly consistent association with item bias is item difficulty (e.g., Kok, 1988; Linn, 1993): More difficult items tend to show more bias. It would be highly ironic to have to conclude that all these psychometrically sophisticated techniques cannot offer more and have merely re-invented item difficulty.

When analyzing item bias, the high level of sophistication of modern conditional methods such as the Mantel-Haenszel and item response theory procedures should be kept in mind. We usually cannot display similar levels of sophistication in other parts of the study; for instance, our item writing technology lags far behind our item bias detection technology.

Statistical Analyses in Cross-Cultural Research

Standardization

Prior to any statistical analysis, it should be decided whether the data need to be standardized, and if so, which standardization procedure is to be used (Leung & Bond, 1989). Culture-level analyses can yield strikingly dissimilar results for standardized and nonstandardized data. Standardization is usually defined as the computation of z scores ($z = [X - M]/S$, in which X is the score to be standardized, M is the mean of the cultural group, and S is its standard deviation). Standardization is defined here more generally and includes both z scores and transformations to other deviation scores such as X/S and $X - M$. The aim of standardization is the reduction or elimination of unwanted cross-cultural differences such as those due to response sets. If scores are standardized per cultural group, cross-cultural differences in means, standard deviations, or both are eliminated.

Such a procedure requires justification because cross-cultural differences in average scores may not be exclusively due to response sets or other unwanted sources, but may reflect valid differences. The justification is usually based on the presumed equality of averages across cultures. For instance, Schwartz (1992), who has transformed raw scores into deviations from the mean in his value survey, argues that the overall average score that people give to all the value items in his inventory should be similar across individuals (and by implication, across cultures), because his instrument is intended to represent a comprehensive set of human values. If such a reasoning cannot be justified, a more prudent approach can be adopted by comparing the structures obtained from standardized and nonstandardized data.

Structure-Oriented Techniques

Manifest behaviors of individuals from other cultural groups often strikes us as being totally different from our own. Such an observation can trigger the question as to whether these differences in manifest behaviors reflect cross-cultural dissimilarities in underlying structures. Do cross-cultural differences in rules for addressing superiors merely reflect cultural variations on the universal need to regulate interactions in hierarchical relationships? Or are the underlying aims so different as to render them incomparable? Do scores on a neuroticism scale have the same meaning across cultures? Or are cross-cultural differences in structure of personality sufficiently large to preclude any meaningful cross-cultural comparison?

A hierarchy of equivalence levels was proposed in Chapter 2 in the section titled Levels of Equivalence. Structure-oriented techniques tend to examine construct equivalence. Together with full-score equivalence, they are the most frequently studied type of equivalence, addressing the cross-cultural comparability of structures underlying behavior. A relatively large set of statistical techniques is available to address construct equivalence: exploratory factor analysis and target (or Procrustean) rotation, structural equation modeling, and—less frequently employed—multidimensional scaling and cluster analysis. All these techniques are discussed below. We will not provide a full-fledged description of each technique, but we will talk on issues that are relevant in testing structure-oriented questions. We will describe how to conduct an analysis when the technique is part of widely available statistical packages.

Exploratory Factor Analysis

Probably the most frequently applied technique for addressing construct equivalence is exploratory factor analysis (Harman, 1976; McDonald, 1985) followed by target rotations and the computation of an index of factorial agreement across cultural groups. The aim of the analysis is to express observed scores (say, scores on an intelligence test) as scores on a limited set of unobserved, underlying factors (such as reasoning, perceptual speed, and memory ability). The relevance of factor analysis for establishing construct equivalence is obvious: Factor analysis decomposes observed scores into these unobserved constituents.

Suppose that a factor analysis has been carried out for each cultural group separately. The similarity of the factor-analytic solutions can then be addressed. Unfortunately, a complication arises in the comparison, known in the factor analytic literature as the "rotation problem": The spatial orientation of factors in factor analysis is arbitrary. Factor solutions obtained in different cultural groups may be rotated with regard to each other. Without such a rotation, the agreement between the factors will be underestimated. So, prior to an evaluation of the agreement of factors in different cultural groups, the matrices of loadings should be rotated with regard to each other so as to maximize their agreement. This is called target rotation. When two cultural groups are studied, one group is arbitrarily designated as the target group. Factor loadings of the second group are rotated toward the target group. The same procedure can be applied when more than two groups are studied; in the latter case, the factor loadings of the separate groups can be rotated either to one target group or to a joint common matrix of factor loadings (a "centroid"). This common matrix is sometimes derived on theoretical grounds. As an example, suppose that a checklist of psychiatric symptoms is administered to a heterogeneous clinical population and that the expected pattern of high and low loadings of symptoms on psychiatric syndromes (i.e., the factors) are known. This matrix can serve as the target matrix.

In other cases, the common matrix is derived mathematically from a factor analysis of the scores of all subjects of all cultural groups. The data are usually standardized per cultural group before the analysis in order to remove unwanted cross-cultural differences in level (e.g., due to response sets). A distorted factor structure may be found without the standardization, particularly when the items (or subtests) show substantial cross-cultural score differences. The correlation matrix of the combined groups will tend to show high values, because one group scores consistently lower than the other group on all items. In a factor analysis the high intercorrelations will increase the size of the first factor. However, the factor may merely reflect aggregation effects and may disappear when the data are standardized prior to the analysis.

After a target rotation has been carried out, factorial agreement can be estimated. The most widely applied statistic is Tucker's coefficient of agreement, also known as Tucker's phi (Tucker, 1951; the formula is presented in Table 4.3). Zegers and Ten Berge (1985) call it the coefficient of proportionality because the coefficient is insensitive to multiplications of the factor loadings (i.e., the coefficient remains identical when all loadings of a factor in a single group are multiplied by a constant) but is sensitive to a constant added to all loadings of a factor. As an example, suppose that the factor loadings of three items in one group are .20, .30, and .40, and in a second group (after target rotation) .40, .60, and .80. Because the two sets have a perfect multiplicative relationship, Tucker's coefficient will be equal to one. Other agreement indices can be envisaged (Zegers & Ten Berge, 1985; see Table 4.3). The identity coefficient is the most stringent statistic, being influenced both by additive and multiplicative transformations. The least stringent is the linearity coefficient (the classical product-moment correlation); it is influenced by neither addition nor by multiplication. The proportionality and additivity coefficient occupy intermediate positions.

Which index should be chosen in applications of exploratory factor analysis? Instead of opting for a single index, a more pragmatic stance is to report all indices and compare their values (see van de Vijver & Poortinga, 1994). This will give a more detailed picture of the factorial similarity than can be obtained on the basis of a single index. When all indices are high, there is strong evidence that the same factor is measured across cultures. When low values are found or when large differences between indices are observed (e.g., a much lower value for the

TABLE 4.3 Overview of Coefficients for Evaluating Factorial Agreement After Target Rotation and Their Susceptibility to Linear Transformations

Coefficient	Influenced by Multiplications	Influenced by Additions	Computational Form
Identity	yes	yes	$e_{xy} = 2\Sigma \dfrac{x_i y_i}{\Sigma x_i^2 + \Sigma y_i^2}$
Additivity	yes	no	$a_{xy} = \dfrac{2s_{xy}}{s_x^2 + s_y^2}$
Proportionality (Tucker's coefficient)	no	yes	$p_{xy} = \dfrac{\Sigma x_i y_i}{\sqrt{\Sigma x_i^2 y_i^2}}$
Linearity (correlation coefficient)	no	no	$r_{xy} = \dfrac{s_{xy}}{s_x s_y}$

NOTE: s_x = the standard deviation of x; s_y = the standard deviation of y; s_{xy} = covariance of x and y.

identity index than for the correlation coefficient), the universality of the factors can be questioned. An inspection of the differences in factor loadings in the cultural groups and an examination of the reasons for the discrepancy are called for.

Most of the indices in Table 4.3 do not have known sampling distributions; hence, it is impossible to establish confidence intervals. Some rules of thumb have been proposed. Values higher than .95 are seen as evidence for factorial similarity, whereas values lower than .90 (van de Vijver & Poortinga, 1994) or .85 (Ten Berge, 1986) are taken to point to nonnegligible incongruities. These values are adequate when we are interested in the evaluation of factorial similarity at a molar level: Are similar factors represented in both cultural groups? When we are interested in a more detailed comparison of the similarities and differences of the factor compositions, however, these values may be too low. Monte Carlo studies have shown that factors that are identical except for one or two (biased) items can show values well over .95 (Bijnen, Van der Net, & Poortinga, 1986; van de Vijver & Poortinga, 1994). As an example, the target rotations that were used in studies with the Eysenck personality questionnaires (which are somewhat different from the procedure mentioned above; see, e.g., Eysenck & Eysenck, 1983) have been criticized as insufficiently powerful to detect anomalous items. Bijnen et al. (1986; Bijnen & Poortinga, 1988) have shown that high agreement indices can be obtained for matrices of factor loadings with only moderately similar values. Eysenck's (1986) counterargument that chance alone cannot explain the high agreement indices is not entirely to the point (see Eysenck, Barrett, & Eysenck, 1985). The issue is not whether chance alone can produce high agreement indices, but whether inappropriate items are detected by the procedure adopted. More powerful techniques (such as confirmatory factor analyses, discussed below) will provide statistically more appropriate tests of the universality of the structure underlying the Eysenck Personality Questionnaire.

In sum, these indices are sufficiently accurate to examine factorial similarity at a global level but not accurate enough to identify anomalous items and subtle differences in the factorial composition and meaning across groups. In empirical applications, a visual comparison of the target loadings and source loadings (after target rotation) is needed to identify discrepancies, irrespective of the value of the index.

It is unfortunate that programs for target rotation, a statistical technique that is so important to cross-cultural research, are not available in common statistical packages such as SPSS and BMDP. Most programs for target rotation are available only on main frames; only a few programs run on personal computers (e.g., the Procrustes-PC program, Dijksterhuis & Van Buuren, 1989). Computer programs with extensive facilities for matrix manipulations usually also have procedures for target rotations. McCrae, Zonderman, Costa, Bond, and Paunonen (1996) provide a routine for carrying out target rotations for the statistical package SAS. An SPSS program is described in Box 4.8.

We will give a few examples of the rich literature on the use of exploratory factor analysis in cross-cultural research. Vandenberg and Hakstian (1978) factor analyzed 50 test scores based on samples of 10- to 12-year-old Scots, Ugandans, Eskimos, and Canadian Indians. One common target matrix was composed, with seven factors, four of which showed moderately high congruence coefficients (verbal-acculturation, ideational fluency, Piagetian conservation, and spatial-perceptual-motor skills). Factorial stability of cognitive tests in cross-cultural applications has often been observed (e.g., Irvine, 1969, 1979).

An example of a personality measure that has been studied in various cultural groups is the UCLA Loneliness Scale. Factor analyses have

BOX 4.8
An SPSS Program to Carry Out Target Rotations

The following procedure carries out a target rotation and evaluates the correspondence between the original and the target-rotated factor loadings (see Wrigley & Neuhaus, 1955). One cultural group is (usually arbitrarily) designated as the source group and the second as the target group. The user has to insert factor loadings (rotated or unrotated) for at least two factors obtained in two groups. Both the input and output are shown. The routine is an adaptation of a procedure provided by Robert McCrae.

The input of the program is as follows:

```
MATRIX.
COMPUTE LOADINGS={
    .78,       .10,     -.08,      .15,     -.15;
    .83,      -.03,      .01,     -.48,     -.08;
<Insert target loadings here separated by commas and
each line ended by a semicolon (except for the last one)>
}.
COMPUTE     NORMS = {
    .81,       .02,     -.01,     -.01,     -.10;
    .63,      -.03,      .01,     -.48,     -.08;
<Insert source loadings here separated by commas and
each line ended by a semicolon (except for the last one)>
}.
COMPUTE S=T(LOADINGS)*NORMS.
COMPUTE W1=S*T(S).
COMPUTE V1=T(S)*S.
CALL EIGEN (W1,W,EVALW1).
CALL EIGEN (V1,V,EVALV1).
COMPUTE O=T(W)*S*V.
COMPUTE Q1=O &/ABS(O).
COMPUTE K1=DIAG(Q1).
COMPUTE K=MDIAG(K1).
COMPUTE WW=W*K.
COMPUTE T1=WW*T(V).
```

```
COMPUTE PROCRUST=LOADINGS*T1.
COMPUTE CMLM2=T(PROCRUST)*NORMS.
COMPUTE CA=DIAG(CMLM2).
COMPUTE CSUM2M1=CSSQ(PROCRUST).
COMPUTE CSUM2M2=CSSQ(NORMS).
COMPUTE CSQRTL1=SQRT(CSUM2M1).
COMPUTE CSQRTL2=SQRT(CSUM2M2).
COMPUTE CB=T(CSQRTL1)*CSQRTL2.
COMPUTE CC=DIAG(CB).
COMPUTE CD=CA&/CC.
COMPUTE FACCONGC=T(CD).
COMPUTE RM1M2=PROCRUST*T(NORMS).
COMPUTE RA=DIAG(RM1M2).
COMPUTE RSUM2M1=RSSQ(PROCRUST).
COMPUTE RSUM2M2=RSSQ(NORMS).
COMPUTE RSQRTL1=SQRT(RSUM2M1).
COMPUTE RSQRTL2=SQRT(RSUM2M2).
COMPUTE RB=RSQRTL1*T(RSQRTL2).
COMPUTE RC=DIAG(RB).
COMPUTE FACCONGR=RA&/RC.
COMPUTE CROSS1=PROCRUST&*NORMS.
COMPUTE SUMCROSS=CSUM(CROSS1).
COMPUTE MSSQPROC=CSSQ(PROCRUST)/NROW(PROCRUST).
COMPUTE MSSQNORM=CSSQ(NORMS)/NROW(NORMS).
COMPUTE PROP=SUMCROSS/(SQRT(MSSQPROC&*MSSQNORM)).
COMPUTE CROSS2=SUMCROSS/NROW(PROCRUST).
COMPUTE MEANPROC=CSUM(PROCRUST)/NROW(PROCRUST)).
COMPUTE SDPROC=SQRT(MSSQPROC-MEANPROC&*MEANPROC).
COMPUTE MEANNORM=CSUM(NORMS)/(NORMS)).
COMPUTE SDNORM=SQRT(MSSQNORM - MEANNORM&*MEANNORM).
COMPUTE COVAR=SUMCROSS/NROW(PROCRUST)-MEANNORM&*MEANPROC.
COMPUTE CORREL=COVAR/(SDPROC&*SDNORM).
COMPUTE ADDIT=2*COVAR/(SDNORM&*SDNORM + SDPROC&*SDPROC).
COMPUTE IDCOEF=2*SUMCROSS/(CSSQ(PROCRUST)+CSSQ(NORMS)).
COMPUTE ROWSQDIF=SQRT(RSSQ(PROCRUST-NORMS)/NROW(PROCRUST)).
COMPUTE COLSQDIF=SQRT(CSSQ(PROCRUST-NORMS)/NROW(PROCRUST)).
```

(continued)

BOX 4.8 Continued

```
COMPUTE DIF={PROCRUST-NORMS}.
PRINT PROCRUST /TITLE = "FACTOR LOADINGS AFTER TARGET
ROTATION" /FORMAT F5.2.
PRINT  DIF  /TITLE = "DIFFERENCE IN LOADINGS AFTER TARGET" +
"ROTATION"  /FORMAT F5.2.
* The following two vectors express the difference between
* source loadings and target-rotated loadings. In the first
* vector, the difference is taken between the loadings
* of two corresponding loadings and the difference is
* squared. For each item the squared differences are summed
* across all factors. The square root of these differences is
* then taken. The second vector adds the squared differences
* across variables for each variable.
PRINT ROWSQDIF /TITLE ="SQUARE ROOT OF THE MEAN SQUARED"
+ " DIFFERENCE PER VARIABLE (ITEM)" /FORMAT F5.2.
PRINT COLSQDIF/TITLE ="SQUARE ROOT OF THE MEAN SQUARED"
+ " DIFFERENCE PER FACTOR"  / FORMAT F5.2.
PRINT IDCOEF/TITLE = "IDENTITY COEFFICIENT PER FACTOR"
/FORMAT F5.2.
PRINT ADDIT/TITLE = "ADDITIVITY COEFFICIENT PER FACTOR"
/FORMAT F5.2.
PRINT FACCONGC/TITLE = "PROPORTIONALITY COEFFICIENT PER"
+ " FACTOR" /FORMAT F5.2.
PRINT CORREL/TITLE = "CORRELATION COEFFICIENT PER FACTOR"
/FORMAT F5.2.
END MATRIX.
```

shown that the scale has a stable unifactorial structure among Anglo American and Mexican American adolescents (Higbee & Roberts, 1994), South African students (Pretorius, 1993), and Zimbabwean adolescents and adults (Wilson, Cutts, Lees, Mapungwana, & Maunganidze, 1992).

That not all measures yield stable factors in cross-cultural comparisons is poignantly illustrated in studies of locus of control. In a review of these studies, Dyal (1984) reports a lack of stability of factors in

The (edited) output of the procedure is as follows:

```
Run MATRIX procedure:
FACTOR LOADINGS AFTER TARGET ROTATION
    .78    .15   -.07    .17   -.12
    .84    .02    .00   -.47   -.09

    ........
DIFFERENCE IN LOADINGS AFTER TARGET ROTATION
   -.03    .13   -.06    .18   -.02
    .21    .05   -.01    .01   -.01

    ...................
SQUARE ROOT OF THE MEAN SQUARED DIFFERENCE PER VARIABLE (ITEM)
    .10
    .10

    ........
```

Comment: For each variable (item) differences of the loadings (–.03, .13, . . .) are squared and averaged for all factors. The square root of this average is reported. Low values indicate a good correspondence.

```
SQUARE ROOT OF THE MEAN SQUARED DIFFERENCE PER FACTOR
    .05    .21    .14    .15    .06
```

Comment: The same procedure is followed for the difference per factor (–.03, .21, . . .).

```
IDENTITY COEFFICIENT PER FACTOR:          .99 .80 .85 .91 .99
ADDITIVITY COEFFICIENT PER FACTOR:        .99 .76 .81 .90 .99
PROPORTIONALITY COEFFICIENT PER FACTOR:   .99 .81 .88 .92 .99
CORRELATION COEFFICIENT PER FACTOR:       .99 .77 .84 .91 .99
```

Comment: The meaning of the agreement coefficients is explained in Table 4.3.

popular locus of control scales such as Rotter's IE scale, even among closely related cultural groups. Van Haaften and van de Vijver (1996) administered Paulhus's Locus of Control Scale (see Paulhus & Van Selst, 1990), measuring intrapersonal, interpersonal, and sociopolitical aspects among illiterate Sahel dwellers. The three scales could not be identified in a factor analysis.

The personality measure that has been most frequently studied in cross-cultural research is undoubtedly the Eysenck Personality Questionnaire, measuring psychoticism, extroversion, neuroticism, and social desirability. An overview of the cross-cultural studies can be found in Eysenck and Eysenck (1983). The claimed high factorial agreement of all factors across various cultural groups is weakened, as argued before, by the improper method of assessing factorial similarity.

The widespread use of factor analysis in cross-cultural research has not led to standard procedures for applying the technique. From a methodological perspective, many studies reporting exploratory factor analyses in cross-cultural research suffer from major shortcomings. First, it is common that solutions are compared that were not target rotated. Such comparison will show an underestimation of factorial similarity across cultures. In some applications a target rotation will not increase the agreement indices much and a coefficient of factorial agreement is already high, even before target rotation. However, especially when one or more factors are somewhat differently structured across cultures, target rotation is needed to explore this difference. For example, Schmidt and Yeh (1992) examined the structure of leader influence among Australian, English, Japanese, and Taiwanese managers and compared the findings to data from a study of 357 managers in the United States. The authors claim the cross-cultural similarity of factors and a dissimilarity of behaviors defining the factors. The same leader influence strategies (factors) are used in all countries (such as bargaining, using authority, and sanctioning), but the behaviors defining these leader influence strategies are not identical across cultures. The authors did not carry out a target rotation. Therefore, the similarity of the behaviors defining the factors could be underestimated. Second, many studies do not report an index of factorial congruence such as Tucker's phi. The use of a statistical procedure is better for evaluating factorial agreement than is a visual inspection of the loadings. Finally, applications in which discrepancies between factor analytic solutions are scrutinized at item level are scarce. A fuller exploitation of the possibilities of exploratory factor analysis may well lead to better-founded statements about cross-cultural similarities and differences.

Recently, an interesting extension of exploratory factor analysis has been proposed: simultaneous components analysis (Kiers & Ten Berge, 1989; Millsap & Meredith, 1988). Whereas exploratory factor analysis as discussed here is based on a factor analysis in each cultural group separately, followed by a target rotation and an evaluation of the fit, simultaneous components analysis considers all groups at once. A single set of principal components for all groups is estimated that maximizes the proportion of variance over all groups. Because the principal components are identical across groups, there is no need to evaluate the agreement as in exploratory factor analysis. The proportion of variance accounted for by the joint principal components will be smaller than the proportion accounted for by groupwise principal component analysis. Examples can be found in Zuckerman, Kuhlman, Thornquist, and Kiers (1991) and Kiers and Ten Berge (1994). A computer program is available (Kiers, 1990).

Structural Equation Modeling

The second statistical technique discussed here is structural equation modeling (the analysis of covariance structures). A theoretical introduction can be found in Bollen (1989; see also Byrne, 1989, 1994; Long, 1983). Structural equation modeling is best seen as a set of versatile data-analytic tools with components of both regression and factor-analytic models. We will focus here on the applications that are most relevant for cross-cultural studies: confirmatory factor analysis, path analysis, and "full structural equation modeling," which incorporates both factor analysis and path analysis.

Confirmatory factor analysis is an extension of classical exploratory factor analysis. Specific to confirmatory factor analysis is the testing of a priori specified hypotheses about the underlying structure, such as the number of factors, loadings of variables on factors, and factor correlations. It is a major advantage of confirmatory factor analysis that a wide variety of hypotheses of cross-cultural similarities and differences, often derived from earlier studies, can be tested (see Watkins, 1989). Such specific hypotheses cannot be tested using exploratory factor analysis.

Tests for goodness of fit are available to evaluate these hypothesized cross-cultural similarities and differences. Unfortunately, the evaluation of goodness-of-fit tests in structural equation modeling is not straightforward. The overall chi-square test of model fit is known to be sensitive to sample size; model violations that are trivial from a substantive point of view will lead to a poor fit in large samples. Various other statistics have been developed (Bollen & Long, 1993); the most frequently reported are presented in Table 4.4. It has become common in reports of empirical studies to present a set of fit statistics and to base conclusions on a combination of their (not always convergent) results. Research on the statistics that have been proposed is needed to evaluate their utility in cross-cultural research, particularly to evaluate the over-all model fit for studies involving many samples.

Cross-validation is an important tool in assessing the plausibility of postulated models in structural equation modeling. When the sample size is large enough, a model can be developed (even without extensive prior knowledge of the underlying structure) and its parameters esti-mated on half of the sample and cross-validated on the other half.

The two most frequently employed computer programs for struc-tural equation modeling are LISREL (Byrne, 1989; Jöreskog & Sörbom, 1988, 1993) and EQS (Bentler, 1992; Byrne, 1994). Technical details for a cross-cultural data analysis are described in the user manuals of the LISREL and EQS programs.

Confirmatory factor analysis in cross-cultural research often amounts to a set of tests of the goodness of fit of increasingly more or increasingly less restrictive models. In the first approach, we start with a lenient model, specifying hardly any similarity across groups, and then increase the number of equality constraints. Earlier models will need to be nested in subsequent models. For example, a test of a model postulating two factors in each cultural group is followed by a test that the variables have the same loadings on the two factors across the groups. The fit of hierarchically nested models can be tested by incre-mental fit indices. The test statistic is the difference in goodness of fit between the more and the less restrictive of the two models; more specifically, the difference in fit between two nested models follows a χ^2 distribution with the number of degrees of freedom equal to the difference between the number of degrees of freedom for the two models. Evaluation of incremental fit is a useful tool to test specific hypotheses of cross-cultural similarities and differences.

The specification of constraints is in principle open to the researcher. In practice, it is common to start with a hypothesis of an equal number of factors across groups (without imposing further equality con-straints), followed by a test of the hypothesis of equal factor loadings.

TABLE 4.4 Schematic Overview of Common Fit Indices in Structural
Equation Modeling

Name	Formula	What Does the Index Test?	Value Recommended for Adequate Fit
Overall χ^2	$N-1$ times the fit function of the specified model	Are residuals of predicted and observed covariances all zero?	Nonsignificant value (problem: statistic is sensitive to sample size)
NFI (Normed Fit Index)	$\dfrac{\chi_n^2 - \chi_m^2}{\chi_n^2}$	Incremental improvement in fit of alternative model relative to baseline model	> .90
GFI (Goodness of Fit Index)	$1 - \dfrac{tr\,[(\hat{\Sigma}^{-1} S - I)^2]}{tr\,[(\hat{\Sigma}^{-1} S)^2]}$	Relative amount of (co)variances in the observed covariance matrix that can be predicted by the model	> .90
AGFI (Adjusted Goodness of Fit Index)	$1 - \dfrac{2(q+1)}{2df}(1 - GFI)$	The same as GFI, but with an adjustment for the number of degrees of freedom relative to the number of variables	> .90
RMSEA (Root Mean Square Error of Approximation)	$\sqrt{\hat{F_0}/df}$	Discrepancy per degree of freedom (lack of fit given a particular number of parameters in the model tested)	< .05
TLI (Tucker-Lewis Index)	$\dfrac{\chi_n^2/df_n - \chi_m^2/df_m}{\chi_n^2/df_n - 1}$	Incremental improvement in fit, adjusted for degrees of freedom in models	> .90

NOTE: N = sample size; χ_n^2 = overall goodness of fit of null model (simplest and most restrictive model); χ_m^2 = overall goodness of fit of alternative model; tr refers to the trace of a matrix; $\hat{\Sigma}$ = predicted covariance matrix on the basis of tested model; S = observed covariance matrix; I = identity matrix; q = number of observed variables; df = degrees of freedom; $\hat{F_0} = Max[\hat{F} - df/(N-1)]$ in which $\hat{F}$ is the minimum of the fit function.

If this model shows an adequate fit, equality of factor covariances (correlations) can be added as another constraint in the next step, while a final step evaluates the fit of a model stipulating equality of factor variances. Instead of starting with a lenient model, it is also possible to begin the search with a highly restrictive model and to relax equality constraints in subsequent models. Goodness of fit is evaluated in the

BOX 4.9
An Example of Confirmatory Factor Analysis

Confirmatory factor analysis is illustrated using a study of the equivalence of a computerized and paper-and-pencil versions of the General Aptitude Test Battery (GATB), a speeded aptitude test consisting of seven subtests (van de Vijver & Harsveld, 1994). The performance of 163 applicants for the Dutch Royal Military Academy on the computerized version of the GATB was compared to the performance of 163 applicants on the paper-and-pencil version. These two groups were matched on age, sex, and general intelligence. The study examined possible psychological differences between the two test versions: Do the computerized and paper-and-pencil versions of the GATB measure the same psychological constructs?

The confirmatory factor analysis tested the goodness of fit of nested (increasingly restrictive) models. From the literature and previous analyses on the data set it was known that a two-factorial solution showed a good fit to the data; the first factor was labeled perceptual speed and the second arithmetic ability. A test of two factors in both groups yielded a fair fit ($\chi^2 = 49.84$, $df = 22$, $p < .01$; RMSEA = .06; TLI = .89). When the factor covariances were held invariant, an almost significant increase of the χ^2 statistic was observed ($\Delta\chi^2 = 7.08$, $df = 3$, $p < .07$). When equality of factor variances across test modes was also imposed, a nonsignificant increase of the χ^2 statistic was found ($\Delta\chi^2 = 10.69$, $df = 7$, ns). However, a final analysis in which factor loadings were held equal across test

same way in this approach. An example of a confirmatory factor analysis is given in Box 4.9.

Examples of confirmatory factor analyses in cross-cultural studies are not numerous. Windle, Iwawaki, and Lerner (1988) investigated the cross-cultural stability of the Revised Dimensions of Temperament Survey among 234 Japanese and 114 U.S. preschool children. Using confirmatory factor analysis, evidence was found for the stability of loadings for each of nine factors (i.e., temperament constructs) of the scale.

Wilson (1988) assessed the perception of school life in Australian and American high school students. A panel of local experts adapted the

TABLE 4.5 Results of the Confirmatory Factor Analysis of the Computerized and Paper-and-Pencil Versions of the General Aptitude Test Battery (after van de Vijver & Harsveld, 1994)

Model	χ^2	df	$\Delta\chi^2$	Δdf	TLI	RMSEA
Equal factor model	49.84*	22	NA	NA	.89	.06
Equal factor covariances	56.92*	25	7.08	3	.89	.06
Equal factor variances	67.61*	32	10.69	7	.91	.06
Equal factor loadings	101.89*	39	34.28*	7	.87	.07

NOTE: TLI = Tucker-Lewis Index; RMSEA = Root Mean Square Error of Approximation.
*$p < .05$.

modes produced a highly significant increase of the χ^2 value of 34.28 ($df = 7$; $p < .00$). In sum, an adequate fit was found for a model postulating the same number of factors of the two test versions; however, a model of equal factor loadings had to be rejected. Subsequent analyses, not further reported here, showed that the fit to the two-factor model was better in the paper-and-pencil than in the computerized version and that simple clerical measures were more affected by computerization than measures that required more general knowledge. Construct equivalence could not be demonstrated; computerization of the test made the GATB psychologically different from its paper-and-pencil version.

originally Australian instrument for a population of students from Louisiana. For example, the item *I feel great* was adapted to *I feel proud to be a student; I think that learning is a lot of fun* became *I am interested in the work we do*. Of the original 28 items, 17 were rephrased. Factor analyses, carried out for each group separately, yielded well-interpretable factors. No factors were similar across the two groups, however. The lack of construct equivalence may be inherent in the concept that was measured, but the many adaptations (as in the above examples) have undoubtedly added to the incomparability. De Groot, Koot, and Verhulst (1994) examined the cross-cultural stability of the Child Behavior Checklist, a measure of child pathology, in the United States and the

Netherlands. Most syndromes (factors) were quite similar across these countries. Finally, Taylor and Boeyens (1991) applied confirmatory factor analysis, among other techniques, to study the adequacy of the South African Personality Questionnaire (SAPQ) among Blacks and Whites in South Africa. Only modest support was found for the equivalence of the constructs in the two samples.

A second important application of structural equation modeling is path analysis, which is a statistical technique to evaluate causal models. Path analysis can be viewed as an elaboration of multiple regression analysis. Unlike the latter, path analysis enables the study of multiple dependent variables. Path analysis also allows for the study of direct and indirect effects. Multiple regression analysis estimates the direct effect of one set of variables on a dependent variable. For example, when intelligence and age are used to predict reading performance, the (raw) regression coefficients of these predictors indicate the change in reading score when intelligence and age are increased by one unit (see Figure 4.3). Path analysis can also examine indirect effects. Suppose that one is interested in predicting current income as a function of intelligence and schooling. The researcher may want to test a model in which intelligence has an influence on schooling, which, in turn, has a bearing on income, but that does not assume a direct relationship between intelligence and income (see Figure 4.3). Path analysis is a flexible tool for testing such causal theories. An introduction to the technique, which is particularly popular in sociology, can be found in Bollen (1989).

Some applications of path analyses have been reported in the cross-cultural literature. For instance, Palisi and Canning (1983) tested models of well-being in England, Australia, and the United States. No support was found for a model stating that people in urban environments would attempt to reduce overstimulation by limiting social contacts. On the contrary, city dwellers had more social contacts than dwellers in rural areas. As another example, Costello (1987) studied the predictive value of a path model relating socioclinical variables to outcome variables after treatment for alcoholism in a therapeutic community among Hispanics and Anglos (Caucasians) in the United States. Different relationships between education and outcome were found in the two groups. Finally, Cross (1995) measured independent and interdependent self-construals of American and East Asian students studying in the United States (an individual with an independent self-construal sees him- or

(a) A path model with only direct effects

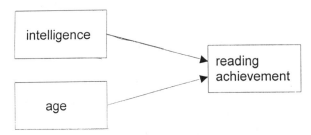

(b) A path model with a direct and an indirect effect

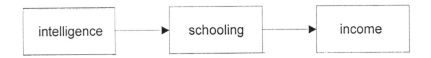

Figure 4.3. Path Models With (a) Direct Effects and (b) Indirect Effects

herself as a bounded entity with own preferences and abilities, whereas with an interdependent self-construal, an individual's identity is defined more in terms of relationships with important others and in-groups). Cross found in a path analysis that among the foreign students, higher scores on the independent self-construal tended to co-occur with high scores on direct coping strategies, which were associated with lower levels of stress. Higher scores on the interdependent self-construal were positively related to increased stress in this group. In the American group, the two types of self-construal, coping, and stress were unrelated.

Path analysis was used in former days to analyze relationships among observed variables (as in Figure 4.3). With the advent of structural equation modeling, it has become possible to include unobserved variables ("full structural equation modeling"). The distinction between regression analysis and (classical) factor analysis has disappeared. Confirmatory factor analyses that aim at unraveling the structure of an instrument can be combined with analyses of the relationships of the construct with context variables such as socioeconomic status; scores on other psychological, educational, or sociological measures; and so on.

Cross-cultural examples of models incorporating both measured and unmeasured variables have also been reported. Homer (1993) studied values and their intergenerational transmission in a sample of U.S. and German parents. She found similarity of value dimensions and differences in transmission of values across the two groups. Reciprocal transmission could be demonstrated for esteem and social values in the United States, whereas this was not found in the German sample. As another example, Brenner and Bartell (1984) studied stress among Swedish and Canadian teachers. A model of the effects of sociocultural factors, life events, and personality on stress showed different relationships in Sweden and Canada. In Canada, life events and personality were more strongly related to stress, whereas sociocultural variables were important in the Swedish sample.

Structural equation modeling has an enormous potential for cross-cultural research that is still largely unrealized (see Singh, 1995). Its flexibility in formulating and adjusting models is an important asset for cross-cultural research. Some caution, however, is required in applying these models—their Achilles heel is often model fit. Models that are based on theoretical considerations may show a poor fit. Computer programs routinely indicate which parameters need to be altered to improve the fit. A mechanistic application of such model modifications can easily lead to a well-fitting model; however, a model that is modified in this way may not survive cross-validation. Moreover, the changes in the model that were needed to obtain a reasonable goodness of fit may be meaningless from a substantive perspective; we may end up with a well-fitting though not interpretable model. As usual, statistical sophistication cannot make up for poor theorizing or instrument design. Model formulations and modifications should be based on substantive considerations, and the tools provided by structural equation modeling can be fully exploited only by a scholarly combination of statistical and substantive considerations.

Confirmatory factor analysis is not meant to replace its exploratory counterpart. When there is not much a priori theory to pose hypotheses about cross-cultural differences and similarities, exploratory factor analysis will be at least as fruitful as confirmatory factor analysis. For example, research on cross-culturally unstable constructs such as locus of control will benefit more from exploratory factor analysis. Only after sufficient cross-cultural evidence has been accumulated to generate hypotheses about cross-cultural differences and similarities can the full potential of confirmatory factor analysis be exploited.

Multidimensional Scaling

Construct equivalence can be examined using multidimensional scaling. Introductions to the technique can be found in Arabie, Carroll, and DeSarbo (1987), Davison (1983), and Kruskal and Wish (1978). Multidimensional scaling attempts to reproduce a matrix of distances between stimuli (e.g., questions of an inventory) in a small number of dimensions that can be meaningfully interpreted. There is an obvious analogy to factor analysis. All data that can be seen as measures of similarity or dissimilarity of stimuli can be subjected to multidimensional scaling, such as Likert-type scales, preference data (e.g., pick k out of n stimuli, or rank orders of stimuli), and dichotomous responses (e.g., yes/no or correct/incorrect). Most multidimensional scaling techniques show the same rotational problem as factor analysis. Distances between stimuli are not affected by (orthogonal) rotations of the axes. Consequently, configurations of such analyses as obtained in different cultural groups have an arbitrary spatial orientation. Target rotations have to be applied prior to an evaluation of the agreement of the solutions. If such rotations are not carried out, the agreement will be underestimated.

Of particular relevance to cross-cultural research is PINDIS, an acronym for Procrustean Individual Differences Scaling (Borg, 1977; Borg & Lingoes, 1987; Commandeur, 1991). PINDIS can be seen as a set of procedures to carry out multidimensional scaling for various cultural groups and to optimize the agreement between the solutions, analogous to the combination of factor analysis and target rotations described previously. The major difference between target rotations in factor analysis and multidimensional scaling is the considerably larger, hierarchical set of procedures in PINDIS to achieve agreement between configurations obtained in different cultural groups. The greater flexibility of PINDIS (as compared to target rotations in factor analysis) is a consequence of the ordinal measurement level of data assumed in PINDIS: More score transformations are allowed at the ordinal level than at the higher measurement levels assumed in factor analysis. A more detailed description of the procedures in PINDIS is given in Table 4.6. These procedures are hierarchically nested; therefore, PINDIS can be used to test hierarchi-

TABLE 4.6   Overview of Names of Models and Their Permissible Transformations in Procrustean Individual Differences Scaling

Similarity Transformation Model: Orthogonal rotation of axes to a common solution, change of origin and measurement unit of dimensions of the separate groups are allowed

Dimension Weight Model One: Above transformations and dimensions of common solution can be stretched or shrunk (weighted) to optimize fit in cultural groups (related to Carroll & Chang's, 1970, INDSCAL model)

Dimension Weight Model Two: Above transformations and dimensions of common solution may be rotated and weighted to optimize fit (related to Carroll & Wish's, 1974, IDIOSCAL model)

Stimulus Weight Model One: Stimulus (instrument) weights (distance from origin to stimulus in common configuration) can vary across cultural groups (different rank orders permitted in different cultural groups)

Stimulus Weight Model Two: Above and origin of each cultural group is allowed to vary. Psychological implications of these transformations have not been addressed

cally nested hypotheses of cross-cultural similarities and differences, analogous to the sequential testing in confirmatory factor analysis that was illustrated in Box 4.9. Yet the structural equation modeling approach allows for a statistically more rigorous test of the fit of the models.

An efficient way to estimate the parameters of multidimensional scaling procedures and to obtain a common solution is the use of dedicated, though not widely available, computer programs for PINDIS models, such as MATCHALS (Commandeur, 1991). A more laborious alternative involves the use of a statistical package to carry out a multidimensional scaling procedure in each cultural group, followed by target rotations. All major statistical packages have facilities to estimate the parameters of multidimensional scaling procedures. For instance, the SPSS package has a procedure called Multidimensional Scaling, part of the Scale procedure. The output configurations from statistical packages can be fed into a program for target rotations, such as the Procrustes-PC program (e.g., Dijksterhuis & Van Buuren, 1989). The SPSS procedure described in Box 4.8 can also be applied to investigate the similarity of multidimensional scaling configurations. It should be kept in mind that most multidimensional scaling techniques have an arbitrary origin and measurement unit of the latent dimensions. This has implications for the choice of agreement index. If both the origin and scaling are arbitrary, the only adequate index in Box 4.8 is the correlation coefficient.

Many applications of multidimensional scaling in cross-cultural research are based on or are at least closely related to facet theory. The theory, developed by Louis Guttman, is a general research methodology that links instrument design to data analysis, usually smallest-space analysis, a nonmetric multidimensional scaling procedure (Canter, 1985; Guttman, 1955; Shye, Elizur, & Hoffman, 1994). The core of facet theory is the so-called mapping sentence, a formal representation of all facets of an instrument. Suppose a researcher wants to construct an arithmetic test. First, a number of facets are identified. Such facets describe stimulus aspects that are assumed to provide an adequate structural definition of the content domain. The first facet of each item may consist of the four arithmetical operations addition, subtraction, multiplication, and division. In facet theory, this is called a facet with four levels. Also, suppose that the researcher wants to use numbers with one, two, and three digits. This constitutes a second facet. By forming the Cartesian product of the two sets (also called crossing), 12 kinds of items can be composed (4 levels of the first facet times 3 levels of the second facet). Responses are scored as correct or incorrect. The mapping sentence specifies the instrument design in facet theory (see Figure 4.4).

We have an unordered and an ordered facet in our instrument (the first and second facets, respectively). Combinations of facets give rise to particular spatial forms in multidimensional scaling solutions, such as circular, cylindrical, wedgelike, and other structures, known as simplex, radex, and circumplex (Canter, 1985; Shye et al., 1994). These structures can already be recognized from the correlation matrix. For instance, a correlation matrix has a simplex pattern if the correlations become smaller when one moves away from the main diagonal. In a circumplex, the correlations first decrease and then increase again when moving away from the main diagonal. A multidimensional scaling applied to such a correlation matrix will reveal a two-dimensional solution with a circular ordering of stimuli. An essential aspect of the data analysis is the recovery of the hypothesized structure. The mapping sentence is taken to provide an adequate theory of the structure of the instrument if the theoretically predicted structure (e.g., a simplex or circumplex) is retrieved in a multidimensional scaling procedure. Other statistical techniques have been proposed more recently to analyze data

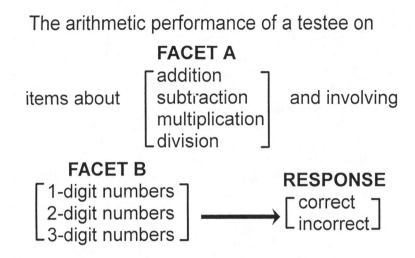

Figure 4.4. Mapping Sentence of a (Fictitious) Arithmetic Task

based on mapping sentences that are also appropriate for retrieving the expected structure, such as structural equation modeling (Mellenbergh, Kelderman, Stijlen, & Zondag, 1979) and item response theory (van de Vijver, 1988).

The close link between theory, instrument design, and data analysis that is characteristic of facet theory is useful in cross-cultural research. It forces a researcher to be explicit about the aspects that are covered by the construct. Inexplicable occurrences of bias, often reported in item bias research, are less likely to be observed with instruments based on facet theory. Moreover, mapping sentences given in reports enable scrutiny of the scope of the instrument by others.

A well-known example of multidimensional procedures in cross-cultural research is Schwartz's (1992, 1994; Schwartz & Sagiv, 1995) analysis of the universality of human values. In his view, the structure of human values can be represented in two orthogonal dimensions, openness to change versus conservation and self-transcendence versus self-enhancement. Ten value types, measured by a total set of 44 values, are distinguished, namely power, achievement, hedonism, stimulation, self-direction, universalism, benevolence, tradition, conformity, and security. These 10 types can be seen as wedges of a two-dimensional structure. Schwartz presented empirical evidence for the cross-cultural stability of the two-dimensional structure across 40 countries. The value structure is taken to apply to a particular cultural group when items are located in the correct value type (wedge). Deviations from the general structure tend to be minor.

Folk taxonomies of emotion words have also been studied using multidimensional scaling. Russell, Lewicka, and Niit (1989; see also Russell & Sato, 1995) studied the perception of similarities and differences in feelings among individuals in Estonia, Greece, Poland, and China. In a previous study with an English-speaking group, two bipolar dimensions were found to provide an adequate description of the data: pleasure-displeasure and arousal-sleepiness. The same two dimensions were found in all other cultural groups.

Some multidimensional scaling models are particularly attractive for cross-cultural researchers because they allow for a fine-grained, simultaneous modeling of cross-cultural similarities and differences. The best known model is INDSCAL (Carroll & Chang, 1970; see Table 4.6). A number of cross-culturally identical dimensions is assumed to underlie a data set (defining the construct equivalence of the measure), but the weights (salience) of these dimensions can vary across cultures. Herrmann and Raybeck (1981) studied the similarity of the structure of terms for common animals (e.g., goat, lion, mouse, and rabbit) and of emotions (e.g., contempt, pride, worry, and guilt) in six locations— Spain, Vietnam, Hong Kong, Haiti, Greece, and the United States (which had three samples, one of which consisted of Native Americans). INDSCAL analyses showed a reasonable fit for two-dimensional solutions for both animal and emotion terms. The animals were classified in all cultural groups along dimensions of size and predatory relationships; the emotion dimensions were pleasantness-unpleasantness and level of activation (see Russell et al., 1989). The appreciable differences that the authors observed in dimension weights across cultures were hard to interpret. They could reflect interesting cultural idiosyncrasies, but the sample sizes in all groups were so small (< 25) that the role of sample fluctuations could not be ruled out. Another example in the cross-cultural literature has been reported by Forgas and Bond (1985). They investigated cultural influences on the perception of common encounters in daily life among 58 students from Hong Kong and 80 students from Australia. The students provided judgments about their implicit representation of 27 social episodes common in both cultures.

Using INDSCAL, salient cross-cultural differences could be demonstrated in the cognitive representation of the encounters.

The two techniques for structure-oriented questions that have been presented so far, factor analysis and multidimensional scaling, are sometimes applied to the same data. A choice between the two techniques is immaterial in many cases because essentially similar structures (factors in a factor analysis and dimensions in a multidimensional scaling procedure) may be found. When the results of the two are not identical, it is common to find that the number of dimensions identified in multidimensional scaling is smaller than the number of factors extracted according to an eigenvalue-larger-than-one or scree-test criterion. In other cases, however, the choice between the two techniques can be critical. When an exploratory factor analysis is carried out on data that are based on mapping sentences, it is common to encounter problems in retrieving the expected structure.

Cluster Analysis

Another technique relevant to cross-cultural research is cluster analysis, to which an introduction can be found in Everitt (1980). The aim of cluster analysis is the classification of multivariate data in a limited set of nonoverlapping categories; each category has some common characteristic that is not shared by members of another category. Despite its relevance for cross-cultural research, there is a paucity of cross-cultural studies applying cluster analysis. Moreover, the methodological problem of comparing cluster analytic solutions across cultures has not been adequately dealt with. After cluster analyses have been carried out in each cultural group separately, a stimulus by cluster matrix can be obtained for each group, indicating which variables belong to which cluster. These dichotomous matrices can be compared across cultural groups, using common agreement indices for nominal data such as Cohen's kappa (1960; Cichetti, Showalter, & McCarthy, 1990). This way of evaluating the cross-cultural stability of cluster-analytic solutions may work well when the number of clusters is small compared to the number of variables. When the number of clusters is large, however, many cells of the indicator matrix will be empty because only a few variables will belong to a cluster. This will lead to an artificial boost of Cohen's kappa. Computer programs for cluster analysis are widely available. All major statistical packages have facilities for carrying out such analyses.

To the authors' knowledge, no applications exist in which clusters obtained in different cultural groups are formally compared to each other to evaluate cross-cultural agreement. A cross-cultural study applying cluster analysis has been reported by Espe (1985). He examined the adequacy of the Graphic Differential as a language-free alternative to the semantic differential (Osgood, Suci, & Tannenbaum, 1957). The original scale uses bipolar adjectives such as "good-bad" and "strong-weak"; the Graphic Differential employs pictorial scales. A previous study among American students revealed the presence of three clusters of the bipolar adjectives in the Graphic Differential. Espe administered the pictorial scales to American and German students; they were asked to sort the figures into nonoverlapping groups. A matrix with the number of co-occurrences between pairs of figures was subjected to a cluster analysis. Three clusters were reported, more or less representing the three factors of the bipolar adjective version: evaluation, potency, and activity. The clusters were largely identical for the two groups, except for a few deviations. For example, whereas in the American sample an arrow pointing up was associated with evaluation, for the German subjects the arrow was more linked to activity. The author concluded that the graphic scales do not fully constitute a language-free, cross-culturally comparable alternative to the bipolar adjective scales.

Level-Oriented Techniques

t Test and Analysis of Variance

The most frequently reported statistical tests for level differences are the *t* test and analysis of variance (e.g., Glass & Hopkins, 1984; Hays, 1994). Their null hypothesis specifies that there are no differences across cultural groups. In a *t* test, cultural group is the independent variable and the score on a psychological instrument is the dependent variable. The popularity of the *t* test, in cross-cultural research as well as in other fields, undoubtedly is due to its simplicity, availability in computer packages, and robustness against violations of assumptions. The same argument holds for the analysis of variance, which is used when data from more than two cultural groups are studied. The focus of this type of analysis is the main effect of culture, which reflects whether the cultures being studied show different means on the dependent variable. Both a *t* test and an analysis of variance require full score equivalence. When the presence of bias cannot be ruled out, the interpretation of such a significant difference may be ambiguous. Observed differences may be due to valid differences or to some form of bias such as method bias (e.g., differential response sets).

More complex designs, so-called factorial designs, are often reported in cross-cultural research. In a factorial design, in addition to culture, one or more independent variables such as gender or age are included. The inclusion of additional variables, such as gender, is relevant when differences on the dependent variable resulting from differences in such independent variables (such as between males and females) vary across cultures. This pattern of results will come out as an interaction effect between gender and culture in the analysis of variance.

There are two approaches to examining interaction effects in a cross-cultural study. The first, addressing level-related questions, is concerned with direct comparisons of a dependent measure across cultures for each level of the independent variable. For instance, Hannover (1995) has studied self-evaluations of teenagers in the former East Germany and West Germany. In addition to culture, academic performance of the teenagers was included as an independent variable. Based on their school grades, the participants were grouped into three performance groups: high, medium, and low. This study employed a 2 × 3 factorial design, with two cultures (East and West Germany) and three performance groups (high, medium, and low) as the independent variables. The dependent variable was self-evaluation of academic achievement. A significant main effect of performance was found, which showed a positive relationship between performance and self-evaluation. A marginally significant culture effect was found, which showed that West German participants were more positive in their self-evaluation than were East German participants. A significant country-by-performance interaction was also found. Analyses for simple main effects revealed that for the high-performance group, there was no difference between the two groups. For the medium- and low-performance groups, the East German participants judged their academic achievement as less positive than did the West German participants. Based on this result and other evidence, Hannover (1995) concluded that East

German participants showed a weaker tendency toward self-protective biases than did West German participants.

An examination of interaction effects can also speak to structure-oriented issues. In this approach, no direct cross-cultural comparison is made. Instead, the effect of the other independent variables on the dependent variable is compared across cultures. The same study by Hannover (1995) can also be used to illustrate this approach. Satisfaction with self was also measured in the study. As with self-evaluation, a 2 (Culture: East vs. West Germans) × 3 (Performance group: high, medium, and low) analysis of variance was performed on this dependent measure. The two-way interaction was significant. Analyses of simple main effects showed that for West German teenagers, self-satisfaction was similar across the three performance groups. For East German teenagers, however, the poorer the performance, the more negative the self-satisfaction. It should be noted that the comparisons made in this analysis of interaction components were not cross-cultural but intracultural. The focus is not whether one cultural group shows a higher mean than the other cultural group, but whether the pattern of results differs across groups (structure-oriented). In the example given, the focus is on how academic performance affects self-satisfaction. The question raised is whether this relationship between the independent and the dependent variables is similar across cultures. See Leung and Lind (1986) for another example of using analysis of variance to investigate a structure-oriented research question.

Regression Analysis

Regression analysis evaluates the influence of one or more independent variables on a dependent variable in terms of the amount of variance of the dependent variable that the independent variable(s) can explain. Regression coefficients express the strength of the relationship between one or more independent variables and a dependent variable. The squared multiple correlation is the amount of variance explained by all the independent variables. This statistic gives an overall evaluation of the success of the independent variables in predicting variation in the dependent variable.

In cross-cultural studies, level-oriented hypotheses involve the dummy coding of the cultural groups. If two groups are involved, one dummy variable is needed, and if there are three groups, two dummy variables are needed. The general rule is that the number of dummy variables needed is one less than the number of cultural groups being studied (Cohen & Cohen, 1975, chap. 5). If the regression coefficient of the dummy variable (in the case of two groups) or the multiple correlation for the set of dummy variables (in the case of more than two groups) is significant, it may be concluded that the cultural groups have different means on the dependent variable.

Regression analysis can be carried out on raw or standardized scores (mean of zero and unit variance). Standardization affects the size of the coefficients but leaves the significance level unaffected. In practice, it has become more common to report standardized regression coefficients, because they are independent of the measurement units of the independent variables.

The choice between an analysis of variance (or a t test) and a regression analysis mainly depends on the measurement level of the independent variables. Nominal- and ordinal-level independent variables are often analyzed in an analysis of variance, whereas predictors based on interval-level variables are usually analyzed with a regression model. Yet the choice is more a matter of convenience than of principle. Both approaches are based on the general linear model. Cohen and Cohen (1975) and Pedhazur (1982) have described how an analysis of variance can be seen as a regression analysis. The independent variables of an analysis of variance are the predictors of a regression analysis. The significance tests of the regression coefficients in the regression analysis (which are t tests) yield similar results to those of significance tests of the analysis of variance (F test). Specifically, the squared t values of the regression statistics are equal to the corresponding F ratios of the analysis of variance.

In cross-cultural applications of regression analysis, we are often interested in the question of whether a single regression equation can capture the relationship between the independent and dependent variable in each group. Some regression programs in statistical packages such as P1R in BMDP and computer programs for structural equation modeling can test the null hypothesis of equal regression equations. If these programs are not available, the tests can also be carried out by entering culture as a dummy variable in the regression equation.

This approach is illustrated with two variables (X and Y). The first step in this technique is to obtain a pan-cultural regression equation of

Y on *X*, in which data from all cultures are included. In the second step, culture is added as a dummy variable, and another regression analysis is carried out including as predictors *X*, the dummy variable, and the interaction of *X* and the dummy variable. The multiple correlations of the two equations are then tested for equality. If there is no significant difference between these two multiple correlations, it is concluded that the relationship holds within each culture and across cultures and that the regression weights and the intercepts of the equations are similar in all the cultural groups studied. A significant difference of the two multiple correlations points to the presence of cross-cultural differences on the dependent variable not explained by *X* (for an elaboration of this approach, see Cohen & Cohen, 1975, chap. 8).

Leung (1987) has provided an example of this approach in a study of preference for conflict resolution procedures in the United States and Hong Kong. Two samples, students and adults, were used in each of the two cultural groups. He found that the preference for a conflict resolution procedure was determined by four factors: control, animosity reduction, favorability, and fairness. *Control* refers to the extent to which a procedure is seen as granting the disputants control in the control resolution process. *Animosity reduction* refers to the extent to which a procedure is seen as capable of reducing the animosity between the disputants. *Favorability* refers to the extent to which a procedure is seen as being favorable to the disputant. Finally, *fairness* refers to the extent to which a procedure is seen as fair. In the regression analysis, procedural preference is the dependent variable, and the four factors are the predictors or independent variables. The research question posed was whether the relative importance of these four factors in determining procedural preference might vary across the two cultural groups studied. In other words, the beta weights (standardized regression coefficients) for these factors in the regression equation may be different for the two cultural groups. To explore this possibility, a set of regression analyses was conducted. The following steps were carried out:

1. The four samples were combined (after having first established that there were no overall cross-cultural differences on procedural preference), and the procedural preference ratings were regressed on the four factors. The squared multiple correlation (R^2) for this overall regression equation was found to be .328.

2. Two dummy variables, one for the nature of the sample and the other for culture, were created. Eight variables representing the interactions of the two dummy variables and the four factors were also created. The procedural preference ratings were then regressed on the four factors, the two dummy variables, and the eight variables representing the interactions. The resulting R^2 was found to be .342.

3. The R^2 of the second equation was compared with that of the first equation. An F test indicated that the two R^2s were not significantly different from each other. It was concluded that the regression coefficients for the four factors were similar across the two cultural groups and across the two types of participants.

The more a conflict resolution procedure is seen as favorable to a disputant, as fair, as capable of animosity reduction, and as allowing the disputant control over the conflict resolution process, the higher is the preference for the procedure.

External Validation

One important question that is relevant to all structure- and level-oriented studies is how the cultural differences that were observed can be explained. The most important statistical techniques to answer this question are covariance and regression analysis. Both types use context variables to examine to what extent the differences observed can be accounted for by context variables (covariates). These variables can provide convincing answers to this question by (a) evaluating the hypothesized antecedents of cultural differences and (b) screening out confounding variables. After a brief presentation of the analysis of covariance, both functions will be further discussed in the following sections.

Analysis of Covariance

The analysis of covariance is an extension of the t test and analysis of variance. Like these two, the analysis of covariance tests the presence of intergroup differences on a dependent variable. However, another variable is added in the analysis of covariance, called the covariate, or, in our terminology, the context variable. This variable, which should show the same linear relationship with the dependent variable in each group, is meant to provide an alternative explanation of at least a part of the cross-cultural differences that are expected. For example, suppose that we are interested in a cross-cultural study of subjective well-being and that we want to control for cross-cultural differences in income. An analysis of variance comparing average well-being scores of various groups will confound differences in well-being and differences in income. The analysis of covariance disentangles national and income differences; it tests cross-national differences on scores that are statistically corrected for income differences. The statistical correction can be seen as an alternative to experimental control. Covariance analysis is highly useful in cross-cultural research because of the frequent presence of such experimentally uncontrollable differences (see Chapter 3, Sampling of Subjects).

Analysis of covariance assumes identical regression coefficients across cultural groups ("homogeneity of regression"). This means that if the covariate is treated as a predictor and the dependent variable as the outcome variable in a regression analysis, then the regression coefficients obtained should be similar across the cultural groups. This assumption can be checked by an F test (Keppel, 1982, chap. 22) or Box M test (see also Cohen & Cohen, 1975, chaps. 10 & 12, and Pedhazur, 1982, chap. 12). The accuracy of the assumption should be checked in every covariance analysis. The conclusions of an analysis of covariance may be misleading if the assumption of homogeneity of regression is violated (see Lord, 1967).

The analysis of covariance is available in all statistical packages. An example of an analysis of covariance is given in Box 4.10. We encourage the use of covariates because they provide an effective way to confirm a particular interpretation of cross-cultural differences or to falsify alternative interpretations. Nevertheless, the limitations of methodological and statistical procedures should be acknowledged. Statistical techniques can only help to evaluate the impact of context variables— they do not provide information on which covariates to choose. For example, cultural differences in performance on cognitive tests may be related to educational quality in a society, means of subsistence, and wealth, just to mention a few possibilities, all of which may be included as covariates. Methodological and statistical considerations cannot help us decide which covariates to include, and we need an explicit theoretical framework or at least some educated guesses to help us make this decision.

BOX 4.10
Analysis of Covariance

The BMDP program P1V is used to carry out an analysis of covariance. The independent variable is called CULTURE, the covariate COVAR, and the dependent variable DEP_VAR.

The input of the program is as follows:

```
/VARIABLE  NAMES = CULTURE, DEP_VAR, COVAR.
/GROUP     VARIABLE = CULTURE. CODES(CULTURE) = 1, 2.
           NAMES(CULTURE) = 'Group A', 'Group B'.
/DESIGN    DEPENDENT = DEP_VAR. COVARIATES = COVAR.
/PRINT     MEANS.
/END
```

The (edited) output is as follows:

```
ESTIMATES OF MEANS

                      Group A              Group B
                         1                    2
CULTURE    1          1.0000               2.0000
DEP_VAR    2          3.5000               4.6667
COVAR      3          4.5000               5.3333
```

Comment: The observed means are printed.

```
COVARIATE        REG.COEFF.   STD.ERR.   T-VALUE   PROB(2-TAIL)
VAR. 3 COVAR      0.66538     0.09382    7.09190    0.000
```

Evaluation of Hypothesized
Causes of Cultural Differences

Context variables can be used to evaluate the interpretation of cross-cultural differences as hypothesized by the experimenter. Poortinga and van de Vijver (1987) have outlined a general procedure for external validation with the use of covariates that is closely related to the analysis of covariance and Leung's (1987) test of the equality of standardized regression coefficients. The procedure presupposes that data are collected in at least two cultural groups. Data should also be collected on additional variables, context variables, that are likely to be

Comment: The regression coefficient of COVAR is given. As can be seen in the last column, COVAR shows a significant regression coefficient.

GROUP	N	GP.MEAN	ADJ.GP.MEAN	STD.ERR.
Group A	30.	3.50000	3.77724	0.25487
Group B	30.	4.66667	4.38942	0.25487

Comment: The columns represent the group names, sample size, observed means, adjusted means (after the impact of the covariate has been removed), and the standard error of the means.

ANALYSIS OF COVARIANCE TABLE

SOURCE OF VARIATION	D.F.	SUM OF SQ.	MEAN SQ.	F-VALUE	PROB
EQUALITY OF ADJ. MEANS	1	5.3631	5.3631	2.8184	0.099

Comment: The F ratio testing the equality of the two group means is not significant (after adjusting for the covariate). The averages of the two cultural groups do not differ significantly.

EQUALITY OF SLOPES

ALL COVARIATES,

SOURCE OF VARIATION	D.F.	SUM OF SQ.	MEAN SQ.	F-VALUE	PROB
ALL GROUPS	1	2.2069	2.2069	1.1631	0.285
ERROR	56	106.2557	1.8974		

Comment: This is the output of the test of the assumption of homogeneous regression. A t test of equality of regression coefficients is not significant ($p = .285$). The assumption appears not to have been violated here.

able to explain cross-cultural differences. The data analysis starts with an analysis of variance to test the null hypothesis of no cultural differences on the dependent variable. Context variables are introduced in the next step; they are used as covariates in an analysis of covariance or as predictors in a regression analysis. In terms of an analysis of variance, the main effect of culture is tested twice: before and after the introduction of covariates. Let us call the corresponding F ratios F_1 and F_2, respectively. If F_1 is not significant, there are no cross-cultural differences to be explained (even though there is still a remote possibility that the introduction of context variables could reveal significant cross-cultural differences). A significant F_1 value points to cross-cultural differences. Context variables will play a central role when F_1 is significant. A comparison of the significance of F_1 and F_2 can yield three possibilities. First, F_1 and F_2 may not differ significantly from each other. In this case cross-cultural differences cannot be accounted for by the context variables. Second, F_1 is significantly larger than F_2 but F_2 is still significant. Context variables are related to the dependent variable. Cross-cultural differences in the dependent variable become smaller after the context variables are controlled, but the differences are still significant. Context variables provide a partial explanation of the cross-cultural differences. Third, after the inclusion of context variables, F_2 is no longer significant. We can then conclude that cross-cultural differences can be accounted for entirely by the context variables.

Hui, Triandis, and Yee (1991) have provided an example of the use of the analysis of covariance design to evaluate the role of individualism-collectivism in explaining cultural differences in reward allocation. The authors compared the distributive behavior of Chinese and American subjects and obtained results consistent with those reported by Leung and Bond (1984). Hui et al. found that when the reward to be divided was fixed, Chinese subjects followed the generosity rule more closely, which led to the allocation of a larger share to the recipient, than did American subjects. That is, they used an equality norm when their input was high, and an equity norm when their input was low; the equality norm specifies an equal allocation of a reward among group members, whereas the equity norm specifies that the share of a member should be proportional to his or her input. In addition, Chinese subjects were found to show a stronger preference for equality than American subjects when the recipient was an ingroup person. When the reward was unlimited, however, Chinese subjects were found to use equality to a larger extent than did American subjects. Using the INDCOL scale developed by Hui (1984) for measuring individualism-collectivism, Hui et al. (1991) were able to see whether individualism-collectivism was in fact related to the observed cultural differences in allocation behavior. When individualism-collectivism was treated as a covariate in an analysis of covariance, the cultural difference in the use of equality disappeared in the case of unlimited resources. This result suggested that collectivism was indeed an adequate explanation of the cross-cultural differences in the use of equality in this condition. In the case of limited resources, however, the cultural differences in allocation still remained significant. The tendency for Chinese subjects to follow the generosity rule and give the recipient a larger share was not adequately explained by individualism-collectivism. This pattern of results led Hui et al. (1991) to conclude that the individualism-collectivism framework may be too global and nonspecific when it comes to explanation or prediction of specific allocation behavior. This example illustrates how the inclusion of individualism-collectivism as a covariate is able to support its role in explaining cross-cultural differences in the use of the equality norm, but the analysis also casts doubt on the role of the covariate in explaining cultural differences in the use of the generosity norm.

Earley (1989) has provided an example of the use of regression analysis to evaluate the effects of a covariate. His study is concerned with the role of individualism-collectivism in explaining cultural differences in social loafing. It is widely documented that Americans show a tendency toward social loafing, which refers to the tendency to exert less effort in a group than when working alone. He argued that this tendency is due to the individualistic nature of American society. In collectivist cultures, there is a heightened distinction between ingroups and outgroups. Collectivists are more concerned with the well-being of the ingroup and hence should not show the loafing phenomenon when they work with ingroup members. In an experiment, Chinese and American management trainees were asked to work as groups. The total output of the group was the dependent variable, and their individualism-collectivism level was measured as a covariate. Hierarchical regression analyses were used to test whether the effect of culture could be explained by the independent variables (i.e., experimental manipulations such as either asking or not asking subjects to put their name on adhesive labels so as to give the impression of accountability of their individual performance) and the covariate. In the regression analysis, the independent variables, the covariates, and all the associated interactions were entered first, and culture was entered as an independent variable in the last step. When the variables were entered in this sequence, culture was found to be nonsignificant. Earley (1989) was able to show that when the effects associated with the independent variables and individual-collectivism were taken into account, cultural difference in social loafing was not significant. The independent variables and individualism-collectivism were able to explain all cultural differences in social loafing.

Control of Nuisance Variables

Context variables can also be used to control for nuisance variables; textbook discussions of covariance analysis always seem to have this usage in mind. The inclusion of nuisance variables as covariates will control for cultural differences that influence the behavior in question but that are not specified by the theory. For instance, if we are interested in comparing food intake (calories) of different cultural groups, we may want to control for body length and height. Longer and taller individuals can be expected to consume more calories. Length and height, the covariates, are not meant to provide an explanation of the cross-cultural differences, but these are nuisance variables that need to be controlled. In a study comparing the delinquent behaviors of adolescents in the United States, Australia, and Hong Kong, it was found that there were substantial differences in the father's educational standing in the three cultures (Feldman, Rosenthal, Mont-Reynaud, Leung, & Lau, 1991). The educational standing of the fathers of the Hong Kong subjects was significantly lower than that of the fathers of the Australian and American subjects. To overcome this problem, an analysis of covariance was used to compare cultural means, with the influence of father's educational standing partialed out.

Multilevel Analysis

Individual- Versus Culture-Level Analysis

At least two levels of analysis are possible in cross-cultural research (e.g., Hofstede, 1980; Leung, 1989; Leung & Bond, 1989). In the culture-level approach, culture is the unit of analysis, and the results obtained are characterizations of cultures but not of individuals. The classic study on values by Hofstede (1980) is based on this approach. There is no assumption with regard to whether relationships found across cultures will hold within cultures. Culture-level analyses may lead to the eco-logical fallacy, the incorrect application of culture-level characteristics to individuals (Robinson, 1950): In each country a proportion of women is pregnant, yet it is obvious that this proportion does not apply at the individual level. Pregnancy at individual level and country level are quite different concepts. Cross-level inferences (i.e., the application of findings from one level to another level) can be fallacious because of a difference in meaning of constructs at the individual and cultural levels.

In the individual-level approach, the individual is the unit of analysis. The relationships between two variables may be different across the two levels of analysis, but it is easier to interpret the results if their equality can be demonstrated. An example can be found in "subsystem validation," in which "hypotheses are examined both intraculturally and cross-culturally, so that explanatory variables may be tested at two levels" (Berry & Dasen, 1974, p. 19). The objective of this approach is to establish that the relationships among a set of variables hold within a culture as well as across cultures. Leung and Bond (1989) called such relationships *strong etic relationships*. As an example, these authors factor analyzed a set of values at both the individual and the culture level. The individualism-collectivism dimension was similar across the two levels of analysis, indicating that it is a strong etic dimension, which applies to individuals as well as cultures.

When results from the two levels of analysis are different, two explanations are possible. First, Leung (1989) suggested that different processes may be involved at the two levels. Some third variable may operate at one level but not the other, so that the results are different. For instance, Markham (1988) found that pay did not correlate with performance within each of a number of work groups. Yet when the work groups were used as the unit of analysis, pay was positively related to performance. Different reward allocation processes were involved in the two levels. The equality norm was used when rewards were distributed within work groups, and the proportionality norm was used for reward allocation across groups.

Second, the meaning of the construct may be different across the two levels, as argued before. Lincoln and Zeitz (1980) found that within a social service organization, professional status of an individual was associated with a larger amount of administrative duties. Different results were obtained when the unit of analysis was at the group level. Across a number of social services organizations, the average professional status of the staff correlated negatively with the average amount of administrative duties. The explanation is that a high professional status at the individual level is closely related to a supervisory role. At the group level, however, a larger number of professional staff resulted in a lower need for supervision, which explains the negative relationship found. Therefore, the meaning of professional status of an individual and the meaning of professional status of a social service organization are quite different.

Hierarchical Linear Models

Hierarchical linear or multilevel models can be used to address data with a multilevel structure (Bock, 1989; Bryk & Raudenbush, 1992; Goldstein, 1987; Lee, 1990). This approach originates from educational settings, in which a multilevel structure is obvious. A student belongs to a certain class, which belongs to a certain school. The school in turn belongs to a certain district. Learning outcome can be studied as a function of variables at all these levels; it can depend on ability and effort at individual level, class size and curriculum contents at class level, and expenditure on education at district level. Traditional statistical procedures such as regression analysis are inappropriate for this type of data because they do not take the multilevel structure of the data into account. Special statistical procedures that can deal with the hierarchical nature of the data have been developed; these procedures address the separate and joint effects of variables at different levels on the dependent measure.

In cross-cultural research, data usually exhibit a hierarchical structure. We believe that the application of hierarchical linear models in these studies is useful in explicating the effects on a dependent variable of individual- and culture-level variables as well as their interactions. The application of hierarchical linear models requires the unpackaging of culture into meaningful dimensions. The usefulness of these dimensions vis-à-vis the individual-level variables is then assessed. For instance, assuming that conformity behavior is affected by individuals' individualism as well as the individualism level of their culture, it would be informative to examine how they relate to each other in their effects on conformity behavior.

To the best of our knowledge, these models have not been applied in cross-cultural research. Computer programs for hierarchical linear programs have recently become available, such as HLM (Hierarchical Linear Modeling, 1992), MLn (Multilevels Models Project, 1994), and VARCL (Longford, 1993). A brief introduction to a two-level model is given in Box 4.11. It is hoped that the brief introduction presented here will encourage cross-cultural researchers to apply this promising tool in their work.

Combinations of Level and Structure Orientations

We have treated structure- and level-oriented techniques to analyze cross-cultural data separately in our presentation. However, the distinction should not be treated as a rigid dichotomy. The differentiation can be quite subtle in some statistical techniques, such as regression analysis. Suppose that educational achievement is predicted on the basis of a set of aptitude tests in various cultural groups and that equality of regression lines is tested. Similarity of regression coefficients involves structural relationships, whereas equality of the intercept would refer to level-oriented relationships.

Primarily level-oriented techniques have also been applied to address structure-related questions, as already illustrated in our discussion of interactions in the analysis of variance. As another example, Buss (1989) hypothesized that male-female differences in mate preferences would be universal in each of 33 cultures he studied. This structure-oriented research question was examined using *t* tests, a typical level-oriented technique. The analyses confirmed the hypothesized gender differences in mate preferences in the cultures studied.

Some structure-oriented techniques can also address level-oriented questions. The best example is a test of differences in mean structures in structural equation modeling. The analysis consists of two parts, the first of which establishes partial or complete similarity of factor structure across cultural groups (a structure-oriented analysis). In the second stage, similarity of factor means can be tested (a level-oriented analysis). Byrne, Shavelson, and Muthén (1989) describe a tutorial example for examining such differences. Cross-cultural examples can be found in Grob, Little, Wanner, Wearing, and Euronet (1996), Little and Lopez (in press), and Little, Oettingen, Stetsenko, and Baltes (1995).

BOX 4.11
Hierarchical Linear Modeling

To illustrate how hierarchical linear modeling can be applied in cross-cultural research, assume that we are interested in predicting life satisfaction of individuals, and the predictor we want to use is self-concept. The following regression equation can be used to represent this individual-level model:

$$Y_i = \beta_0 + \beta_1 X_i + r_i \qquad\qquad [4.11.1]$$

Y_i refers to the life satisfaction score of individual i; X_i refers to the self-concept of individual i; β_0 refers to the intercept, which is the value of life satisfaction when the self-concept is zero; β_1 is the slope of the equation, which refers to the expected change in life satisfaction with a unit change in self-concept; and r_i refers to a unique effect associated with the individual i. It is often convenient to scale X, the predictor, so that the intercept becomes meaningful. A common way to do this is to subtract the mean of X from each score: $X_i - M$, where M is the mean of X. If we substitute $X_i - M$ for X in Equation 4.11.1, the slope remains unchanged, and the intercept will become the mean of Y.

Suppose that we want to examine the relationship between life satisfaction and self-concept in several cultures. It is entirely possible that different cultures have different means on life satisfaction. The relationship between life satisfaction and self-concept may also vary across cultures. To represent this situation schematically, Equation 4.11.1 can be expanded as follows:

$$Y_{ij} = \beta_{0j} + \beta_{1j}(X_{ij} - M_j) + r_{ij} \qquad\qquad [4.11.2]$$

The subscript j refers to culture j. Y_{ij} refers to the life satisfaction score of individual i in culture j; X_{ij} refers to the self-concept of individual i in culture j; β_{0j} refers to the intercept of the equation for culture j; β_{1j} refers to the slope for culture j; and r_{ij} refers to a unique effect associated with the individual i in culture j. If cultures differ in the mean of life satisfaction, β_{0j} will differ across different values of j. If cultures differ in the relationship between life satisfaction and self-concept, β_{1j} will differ across different values of j.

We can now develop a model to predict why cultures differ in life satisfaction and why the relationship between life satisfaction and self-concept varies across cultures. We want to develop a culture-level model to predict β_{0j} and β_{1j}. For instance, we may want to use the economic status of a culture as a predictor for both variables. We may create a dichotomous variable, E, to represent the economic status of a culture. For developing countries, E is equal to 0, whereas for developed countries, E is equal to 1. The following two equations can be set up:

$$\beta_{0j} = \gamma_{00} + \gamma_{01}E_j + u_{0j} \qquad [4.11.3]$$

$$\beta_{1j} = \gamma_{10} + \gamma_{11}E_j + u_{1j} \qquad [4.11.4]$$

In essence, Equation 4.11.3 specifies that the life satisfaction of a culture is a linear function of its economic status. Equation 4.11.4 specifies that the relationship between life satisfaction and self-concept across individuals within a culture is a linear function of the economic status of the culture. If we substitute Equations 4.11.3 and 4.11.4 into Equation 4.11.2, we have the following equation:

$$Y_{ij} = \gamma_{00} + \gamma_{01}E_j + \gamma_{10}(X_{ij} - M_j) +$$
$$\gamma_{11}E_j(X_{ij} - M_j) + u_{0j} + u_{1j}(X_{ij} - M_j) + r_{ij} \qquad [4.11.5]$$

Note that the model specified by Equation 4.11.5 is different from a regular regression model because the random error of the model is of a complex form: $u_{0j} + u_{1j}(X_{ij} - M_j) + r_{ij}$. In regression models, the errors are assumed to be independent. In Equation 4.11.5, however, the errors are dependent within each culture because u_{0j} and u_{1j} are common to all members of the same culture. Such models need to be estimated by special procedures. For details and examples of hierarchical linear models, see Bryk and Raudenbush (1992), Goldstein (1987), and Bock (1989).

5

*Design and Analysis
of Four Common Kinds
of Cross-Cultural Studies*

This chapter contains a description of the sampling of cultures, design, data analysis, and major strengths and weaknesses of the four types of cross-cultural studies described earlier (i.e., generalizability, theory-driven, psychological differences, and external validation studies). A schematic overview is given in Table 5.1.

Generalizability studies test the cross-cultural stability of a theory, an instrument derived from a theory, or a relationship. The choice of cultures is ideally based on random sampling, but practical constraints will almost always prohibit this. Most studies apply convenience sampling to select cultures. When the number of cultural groups studied is sufficiently large, one can in principle approach a random sample. In practice, however, convenience sampling will often lead to an under-representation of non-Western cultures. Systematic sampling is also

TABLE 5.1 Typical Methods and Analyses for the Four Common Types of Cross-Cultural Studies (from van de Vijver & Leung, 1997)

Type of Study	Sampling of Culture	Design	Major Analysis	Major Strength	Major Weakness
Generalizability Study	Convenience	Replication of original study or new study	Structure techniques (e.g., correlations, factor analysis, analysis of covariance structures)	Study of equivalence	No contextual variables included
Psychological Differences	Systematic or convenience sampling	Replication of original study or new study	Both level (e.g., t test and analysis of variance) and structure techniques	"Open-mindedness" about cross-cultural differences	Ambiguous interpretation
Theory-Driven	Systematic (maximize contrast on focal variable)	New study; covariates may be present	Both level and structure techniques	Study of relationship of cultural factors and behavior	Lack of attention to alternative interpretations
External Validation	Systematic	Measures at different levels of aggregation; covariates present	Level techniques	Focus on interpretation of cross-cultural differences	Choice of covariates may be meaningless

SOURCE: van de Vijver & Leung, 1997. Used by permission from Allyn & Bacon.

sometimes applied in generalizability studies. Cultures are deliberately sought in these studies as a critical test of the generalizability of the results obtained. When cultures are systematically sampled, it is important to provide a rationale for the choice of cultures.

The design of a generalizability study is usually a replication of the original study. Special care should be taken to ensure that the instrument and administration procedure can be adequately applied in the new cultural context. In Schwartz's (1992) study, items were added to the original list in some cultures to ensure an adequate coverage of the value domain of the local culture and to avoid construct bias. In other studies, the addition of items may not suffice to prevent construct bias, and more extensive instrument adaptations will be required. The influence of some sources of method bias can be lessened by a careful design, such as an explicit assessment of interviewer effects; other sources are less easily tackled, such as differences in stimulus familiarity or social desirability. Small-scale pilot tests can help to explore the influence of these sources.

The data analysis will often consist of two parts, the first of which replicates the original analysis. There is an emphasis on structure-oriented techniques such as factor analysis (e.g., Irvine, 1979) and multidimensional scaling (Schwartz, 1992). The second part addresses the agreement between the original and the new results. Confirmatory factor analyses and target rotations following exploratory factor analysis can be applied to compute this agreement. An explicit analysis of the equivalence of the data is indeed the major strength of generalizability studies.

When the goals of cross-cultural studies are defined as both delineating and explaining cross-cultural differences, generalizability studies capitalize on the first and often ignore the second. It is rare to find context variables for explaining cross-cultural differences included in these studies. To the extent that these context variables are at the individual level (e.g., gender, socioeconomic status, and age), their omission cannot be recovered. When variables are located at culture (country) level (e.g., Gross National Product and population size), yearbooks of international organizations, such as the United Nations and the World Bank, and the Human Relations Area Files (Barry, 1980) can be used as sources of relevant information. This information can be collected post hoc. In addition, country-level information on context variables is particularly relevant when several cultures are studied. If only a few cultural groups have been considered and no theoretical framework is available to guide the choice of context variables, it may be difficult to choose among the many potentially relevant variables.

Studies of *psychological differences* are often based on a less elaborate theoretical framework than are generalizability studies. In most applications a test, questionnaire, or observation scale has been applied in a Western context and interesting results were obtained. A study in a new cultural context is then launched to explore whether there are cross-cultural differences in the responses to this instrument. In other cases, an instrument is simultaneously developed for two or more cultural groups. The choice of cultures is usually motivated by considerations of convenience, whereas in other cases particular cultural groups are sometimes sought because they represent particular values (usually extreme scores) on a target variable. For example, in a study of meta-memory, one could study illiterate subjects to examine the role of formal education in metamemorial processes.

The design of the study is identical in all cultures in the case of simultaneous development or is a replication of the original design if the test has been applied before. All kinds of bias (construct, method, and item) can challenge the equivalence of data. Compared with the other three types of cross-cultural studies, psychological differences studies are most susceptible to bias because they are usually not based on well-developed theories and do not address alternative interpretations. Therefore, the study of bias requires close scrutiny in all stages of these studies. Issues such as construct coverage, translation accuracy, and applicability of the original administration procedure have to be examined prior to the data collection. A pilot study may be required to scrutinize these issues.

In many psychological differences studies, there is an interest in both structure- and level-related questions. The data analysis therefore often includes a mixture of statistical techniques. Preliminary analyses such as the computation of classical psychometric statistics (reliability) and item bias indices can be carried out to examine the appropriateness of the questions of the instrument across all contexts (see Chapter 4, Preliminary Analyses). Such analyses do not warrant strong statements about cross-cultural differences and similarities. For example, the presence of high reliability for an instrument in all cultural groups does not yet imply the universality of the underlying theoretical constructs. Additional analyses such as exploratory factor analyses followed by target rotations, confirmatory factor analyses, or other multivariate techniques are needed to explore the structure underlying the instrument. In some studies, the analyses end with a comparison of the structure obtained in the cultural groups and an establishment of construct equivalence of the instrument across groups by studying the nomological network of the instrument. In other studies, factor analyses or other techniques for examining construct equivalence are followed by a comparison of mean scores, using *t* tests and analyses of variance. As noted in Chapter 2, Levels of Equivalence, however, the similarity of factor structures is an insufficient condition for scalar equivalence.

Another methodological problem of psychological differences studies is their poor control of Type I errors. Multiple tests of the null hypothesis of no cultural differences may be carried out, and "fishing" for significant differences can easily occur (Cook & Campbell, 1979). Various procedures have been developed to control for Type I errors, such as Bonferroni procedures as well as planned comparisons and post hoc procedures in analyses of variance (Glass & Hopkins, 1984; Hays, 1994). Unfortunately, these procedures are only occasionally applied in cross-cultural research.

A major strength of these studies is their "open-mindedness" about cross-cultural differences. The exploration of cross-cultural differences can provide important clues about cross-cultural differences and similarities, addressing questions such as: What kind of questions or items yield the largest and smallest cross-cultural differences? Is there a pattern in the differences? Are the cross-cultural differences more uniform or less uniform across all items? Do floor and ceiling effects have an impact on the observed differences? Are the score distributions similar across cultural groups? Seen from this perspective, broad-band psychological differences studies are explorations that in many cases are indispensable for providing the background of more focused hypothesis-testing studies in the future.

Theory-driven studies test a theory of cross-cultural differences. The theory stipulates a functional relationship between cultural variables and substantive outcomes (e.g., in psychological or sociological variables). Sampling procedures need to be carried out in a careful way. The sampling of cultures is usually systematic because the cross-cultural differences on a focal variable have to be maximized. Furthermore, subject sampling is also critical because differences in subject characteristics often have to be maximized on a few target variables and minimized as much as possible on all other background characteristics. As a hypothetical example, suppose that male-female differences in gender stereotypes are hypothesized to be smaller in feminine than in masculine cultures. A test of the hypothesis requires (ideally) a set of at least two, but preferably three or more, cultures that differ systematically on the masculinity-femininity dimension. The samples should be as similar as possible on all relevant background characteristics. If education is considered a relevant concomitant variable, a matching procedure could be followed by sampling subjects with similar educational levels. When a complete matching cannot be achieved, a viable strategy to account for relevant background variables may be post hoc correction in an analysis of covariance.

The statistical analysis conducted can be either structure- or level-oriented (Chapter 2, Four Common Types of Comparative Studies). Analyses of (co)variance and t tests are usually applied to test the hypothesized cross-cultural differences.

Compared to studies of psychological differences, theory-driven studies are more systematic. Such studies are designed and carried out to critically test a hypothesis. Consequently, such studies provide powerful tests of theories of cross-cultural differences, which is one of the main goals of cross-cultural research. When the hypothesized relationships are observed, they can often be unambiguously interpreted. Yet putting all of the eggs in one basket comes with a risk: There is a lack of attention to alternative interpretations in these studies. When the hypothesized relationships or differences are not observed, the data at hand do not offer much opportunity for exploring reasons for the negative findings; only post hoc explanations can be put forward.

External validation studies take observed cross-cultural level or structure differences as their starting point and scrutinize these differences either by exploring their antecedents or by testing interpretations of these differences. Exploratory studies are more common. In many cases the data to be analyzed will have a multilevel structure (see Chapter 4, Multilevel Analysis). When knowledge is available as to which cultural variables are related to cross-cultural differences on a target variable, cultures can be systematically sampled. Without such knowledge, convenience sampling is usually adopted.

External validation can also take the form of meta-analyses (e.g., Hedges & Olkin, 1985). A hypothetical example would be a meta-analysis of all intracultural and cross-cultural studies carried out with the Raven Progressive Matrices. A meta-analysis investigates relationships between the average score (e.g., average Raven score) obtained in a country and various characteristics of the country such as expenditure on education per head, average level of education, and average income. All common level techniques are used; in addition, regression models are often applied in meta-analyses: One or more predictors (e.g., country characteristics) are used to explain cross-cultural differences on a dependent variable (e.g., the average Raven score).

It is a major strength of external validation studies that they evaluate interpretations of cross-cultural differences or generate hypotheses about such differences that can later be tested in theory-driven studies. An emphasis on the interpretation of cross-cultural differences is a desirable characteristic of cross-cultural studies. A problem of external validation studies is the choice of context variables. For example, it has been shown several times that the distance from a country's capital to the equator is a good predictor of a wide array of psychological and sociological variables. But what is the theoretical meaning of such a predictor? The observation that distance to the equator is a statistically significant predictor dodges the question of the real determinants of the cross-cultural differences. In general, it may not be too difficult to find a set of culture-level predictors (so-called proxies) that can explain cross-cultural differences on a target variable, but it may be more difficult to come up with an adequate interpretation of the relationship.

We believe that each of the four types of cross-cultural studies have a role to play in the research process. In the initial stage, when not much is known about how a phenomenon varies across cultures and what variables produce the variation, psychological differences and external validation studies will help to identify patterns of cross-cultural similarities and differences, thereby providing the basis for posing a coherent theoretical framework. When a sufficient number of empirical studies are available, theory-driven and generalizability studies can be designed to test these statements.

Psychological differences studies dominate the literature (Leung, Bond, & Schwartz, 1995). This is unfortunate because these studies alone are inadequate for theory building, and their abundance partly explains why theoretical development in cross-cultural research is haphazard and slow. In our view, the methodological problems of psychological differences studies tend to be underrated. When an instrument has been administered in two cultural groups, but no context variables are included and bias has not been examined, the number of alternative interpretations of cross-cultural differences observed is as a rule so large that the value of the study is severely restricted. As discussed previously, a host of procedures are available to limit the number of alternative interpretations. The adoption of these procedures will often result in a transition from broad-band explorations to more focused studies in which theories and previous findings are tested. More theory-driven and generalizability studies are needed for theoretical advances in the field.

6

Conclusions

In the previous chapters, typical problems and pitfalls of cross-cultural research were discussed and solutions proposed. The current
chapter briefly integrates the major methodological issues into eight
statements. Each statement is followed by an explanation. The last
section is devoted to our view on the future of cross-cultural research.

Methodological Issues in Cross-Cultural Research

*Statement 1. Cross-cultural differences
in scores on social and behavioral measures
tend to be open to multiple interpretations.*

When an experimental procedure is used to find out whether a drug
influences reaction time, we usually sample two groups, an experimental and a control group, that are as similar as possible on all relevant

characteristics that could influence reaction time. The drug is administered to one group and a placebo is administered to the control group. When a significant difference between the experimental and control groups is observed, we usually feel safe in concluding that this difference is due to the drug administered.

If we consider culture as a set of experimental conditions, we may be tempted to apply an analogous reasoning and to conclude that culture is the antecedent of observed behavioral differences. There are two problems with such an attribution, however. First, culture is not a meaningful variable from a substantive point of view. The statement "Group A scores higher on mental health measures than does Group B because of the cultures of the two groups" does not convey much information. The obvious next question is to identify which cultural factor(s) can be held responsible for this difference. Culture is an umbrella concept encompassing a host of characteristics, and we need to decompose (unpackage) the concept into more meaningful antecedents. Second, the difference in scores on the instrument may have been caused by measurement artifacts. For example, when two cultural groups are found to have different scores on a questionnaire of collectivism, the groups may show valid differences in collectivism. In addition, various alternative interpretations can be envisaged: (a) at least some of the items describe behaviors or attitudes that do not adequately capture the concept of collectivism in one of the cultures; (b) differential social desirability, acquiescence, or other response sets caused the differences; (c) the groups were not matched on relevant background characteristics such as education and income; (d) the physical conditions of the instrument administration varied across cultural groups; or (e) there were differences in motivation of the samples. In short, there is an abundance of alternative interpretations. How we can guard our studies against such alternative interpretations is considered in the following statements.

Statement 2. Cross-cultural studies should assess in each group the appropriateness of:

a. the constructs examined (construct bias)

b. the administration procedures (method bias)

c. the operationalizations (item bias)

Studies in which data from various cultural groups are compared can be plagued by dissimilarities in constructs or construct-related behaviors (construct bias), administration difficulties such as problems with interpreters (method bias), and item-related anomalies such as poor item translations (item bias) (see Chapter 2, Bias: Definitions, Sources, and Detection). It is unfortunate that bias is often insufficiently addressed in empirical research. The study of bias is not a matter of superfluous luxury but of necessity. One cause of the sluggish progress of cross-cultural research is our readiness to take observed cross-cultural differences for granted. Item bias techniques are less frequently applied in social psychological studies of cross-cultural difference than in educational and cognitive studies. It is difficult to imagine substantive or methodological reasons for the difference. Our larger readiness to accept cross-cultural differences in the personality and social domain than in the cognitive domain may primarily express implicit theories of cross-cultural differences among researchers.

Neglecting construct and method bias will affect the equivalence of results. For example, it is known that religion is an important coping mechanism in some religious groups. When a coping questionnaire in which the role of religion is not measured is used to compare religious and irreligious individuals, statements about the coping mechanisms that are used in these groups yield an incomplete picture. Ignoring item bias may sometimes have less severe consequences; when measures with many items have been administered and only a few items are biased, most structure- and level-oriented analyses will not be strongly affected by the item bias.

Statement 3. A wide variety of
measures can be taken to enhance the
validity of cross-cultural comparisons.

Compared to intracultural studies, cross-cultural research is open to more validity threats (see Statement 1). A large number of tools can be applied to deal with these threats (see Chapter 3, Validity Enhancement).

It is impossible to indicate in general terms which bias source will be more prominent in a particular study and which way of dealing with the bias source is to be preferred. A first, essential step is the awareness that bias can play a role. Knowledge of the construct measured and the cultural groups under study are other prerequisites for developing an adequate notion of where bias can be expected. Various techniques can be applied to detect construct, method, and item bias (described in Chapter 2, Construct Bias, and Implications of Bias for Equivalence, and in Chapter 4, Item Bias Analysis, respectively).

Statement 4. The decomposition of culture into context variables is a methodologically powerful means to corroborate interpretations of cross-cultural differences and to reduce the number of alternative interpretations.

In our view, the aim of cross-cultural studies is both to explore and to explain cross-cultural differences. Most of our past efforts have been directed at the exploration of cross-cultural differences, and their explanation has received less attention. Exploratory studies have created a large body of data that are useful for delineating cultural factors that can account for observed cross-cultural differences; such factors have been labeled context variables (Chapter 1, Cross-Cultural Studies as Quasi-Experiments). By including context variables, hypotheses about causal antecedents of cross-cultural differences are tested, which amounts to unpackaging culture by means of context variables (Chapter 4, External Validation). The proposed shift from the exploration to the explanation of cross-cultural differences has methodological implications. It implies a shift from psychological differences studies to hypothesis testing and external validation studies (Chapter 2, Level and Structure Orientation in the Four Types of Cross-Cultural Studies). In hypothesis testing, cultures are typically sampled systematically, and specific theories of cross-cultural differences are tested. An example is provided in Berry et al.'s (1986) study of the ecocultural framework (see Chapter 2, Level and Structure Orientation in the Four Types of Cross-Cultural Studies). External validation studies often adopt a more exploratory approach and attempt to identify variables at the individual, intermediate (e.g., school, family), or cultural level that can account for observed cross-cultural differences.

The use of context variables offers a broad scope for dealing with alternative interpretations (Chapter 4, External Validation). They are often applied to confirm a particular interpretation of cross-cultural differences. As an example, suppose that one is interested in cross-cultural differences in self-esteem and that an instrument is administered in several groups to measure the concept. As a means of studying cross-cultural differences in social desirability of the measures, the desirability of the self-esteem items is assessed among the same respondents. The desirability measures are the context variables. An evaluation of their relative success in explaining cross-cultural differences on the dependent variable, self-esteem, may be examined. An analysis of covariance may be carried out with self-esteem as the dependent variable and the desirability scores as the covariate. The analysis will provide an answer to the question of to what extent a response set such as social desirability can explain cross-cultural differences in self-esteem.

Context variables can also be used to control for the influence of nuisance variables. Suppose that digit span (short-term memory for digits) is investigated among Welsh and American children. It has been found that length of short-term memory span is affected by the time it takes to articulate the digits; Welsh digits take longer to articulate than English digits. Welsh children have been shown to have shorter digit spans than English children (Ellis & Hennelly, 1980). To compare the digit spans of Welsh and American children, differences in articulation time in Welsh and English will have to be controlled. In this application, a covariate (e.g., a measure of the articulation time) is used to control for a nuisance variable.

Context variables constitute a testable framework for the interpretation of cross-cultural differences. Statistical tests can be carried out to evaluate the effectiveness of these variables in the explanation of cross-cultural differences. A testable framework is not always present in validity-enhancing techniques. For example, suppose that a lengthy introduction or learning period has been used in a mental test to reduce differential stimulus familiarity as a nuisance variable in a cross-cultural study. It is uncommon to make an assessment of the success of the instruction intended to reduce the differential familiarity. Yet without such an assessment, it is impossible to evaluate the effectiveness of the lengthy introduction. From a methodological perspective, it will often be preferable to include a measurement of the familiarity as a context variable and to use this measure as a covariate.

Statement 5. Equivalence should
be established and cannot be assumed.

When an instrument has been applied in different cultural groups, it cannot be assumed that the meaning of the score obtained is identical across these groups and that scores can be compared across groups. Cross-cultural comparisons are interpretable only when evidence is given for the equivalence of the measures. In Chapter 2, we introduced different types of equivalence. First, construct inequivalence refers to inequality of constructs across cultures. Construct equivalence implies identity of construct, although the constructs may be measured in different ways in each culture. The second type of equivalence is called measurement unit equivalence and applies to interval- and ratio-level scales. The measurement unit is identical in both groups, whereas origins of the scales differ. The last (and highest) level of equivalence has been labeled scalar equivalence or full score comparability. It assumes measurement on the same interval or ratio scale in each group.

The presence of bias will often challenge the equality of meaning and the comparability of scores. It is unfortunate that this notion is often overlooked. The comparison of means of cultural groups in a *t* test or analysis of variance assumes scalar equivalence. It is uncommon, however, to find evidence to substantiate the claimed equivalence. Without a check on bias, it is difficult to maintain full score equivalence and to interpret significant cross-cultural differences unambiguously.

Statement 6. Higher levels of equivalence
are more difficult to establish.

The most frequently studied levels of equivalence are structural and scalar equivalence. The first kind is usually established using multivariate techniques such as factor analysis. Various statistical techniques are available to test the cross-cultural similarity of the structure underlying an instrument (see Chapter 4, Structure-Oriented Techniques). Scalar equivalence is more difficult to achieve, because it assumes a high measurement level of the scales in each group, and any bias will invalidate this type of equivalence. It is easier to demonstrate that the same constructs are measured across cultural groups than to demonstrate that the instruments yield the same interval- or ratio-level scale across cultures.

Statement 7. The interpretability of cross-cultural research is optimized by a combination of substantive, methodological, and statistical considerations.

Some cross-cultural studies emphasize substantive issues, whereas others focus more on methodological rigor. We strongly believe that these two perspectives are complementary. Theoretical and methodological considerations can strengthen each other. Theory, design, and data analysis can be seen as the links of a chain: They need to be firmly attached to each other, and the weakest link defines the strength of the chain. For example, design and data analysis cannot remedy basic flaws in theory or instrumentation. Construct underrepresentation cannot be overcome by statistical analysis, however sophisticated.

Collaboration between methodologically and substantively oriented colleagues could prove an effective means for arriving at a balance between these two aspects. For instance, in the early stages of an empirical project, it is usually quite easy to forecast or at least generate educated guesses as to which types of biases can be expected. Validity-enhancing techniques can be implemented and context variables can be included in the study to maximize the interpretability of cross-cultural differences. These techniques are to be preferred over a post hoc explanation of the causes of cross-cultural differences. It is easier to prevent than to cure.

Statement 8. Cross-cultural research is essential in establishing the generalizability of theories and empirical results.

Psychological theories that have shown validity in one cultural context do not necessarily yield equally good results in other cultural contexts. For example, Amir and Sharon (1987) have shown that theories of American experimental social psychology had only moderate validity in Israel. Cross-cultural research can help to specify the universality of theories and findings. It is one of the main messages of cross-cultural research that it is naive to assume universality and that research in a single culture can seldom shed light on the cultural limitations of theories and findings.

A plea for cross-cultural research is not meant to indicate that all theories developed in one country are bound to have a low validity elsewhere. We do not maintain such a relativist position. Rather, the cross-cultural generalizability of theories (external validity) requires empirical demonstration. The study of cultural factors should become a routine procedure in developing and testing theories and instruments. It has become a standard practice that data on reliability and validity are reported in the publication of a new instrument. It is hoped that it will also become a standard practice to report cultural variations in instrument manuals. No theory or instrument can claim any appropriateness in a cross-cultural context without reporting such data.

Future Outlook

Cross-cultural research examines the cultural generality of theories and findings. The relevance of the cultural dimension is increasingly appreciated. In fact, we may be starting a new phase of cross-cultural research. In the pioneering phase, cross-cultural research was done by researchers who devoted their careers to the study of cross-cultural similarities and differences. In the current phase, cross-cultural research has gained momentum. Most cross-cultural research is carried out by scholars who study cross-cultural variations as a natural extension of their earlier intracultural work. These scholars usually do not pursue a career in cross-cultural research and after one or more cross-cultural studies, they may want to return to intracultural work. We find this an important development because it demonstrates that interest in cultural variation becomes part and parcel of the scientific enterprise in the social and behavioral sciences. We are optimistic about the future of cross-cultural research. We believe that we are entering into a stage in which our theoretical and methodological sophistication allows us to tackle important problems and produce valid, replicable, and useful results and to delineate the cultural factors in human behavior more precisely. In this book, we have provided an overview of various strategies that can be applied in a cross-cultural study to ensure interpretability and validity of results. However, methodological sophistication is not enough; good theories and conceptualizations should accompany sound methodology. We hope that future cross-cultural work will benefit from improved theorizing and methodology, and as a result will play a central role in the development of truly universal knowledge.

References

Almagor, M., Tellegen, A., & Waller, N. G. (1995). The big seven model: A cross-cultural replication and further exploration of the basic dimensions of natural language trait descriptors. *Journal of Personality and Social Psychology, 69*, 300-307.

Altbach, P. G., Arnove, R. F., & Kelly, G. P. (Eds.). (1982). *Comparative education.* New York: Macmillan.

Amir, Y., & Sharon, I. (1987). Are social psychological laws cross-culturally valid? *Journal of Cross-Cultural Psychology, 18*, 383-470.

Andersen, E. B. (1973). A goodness of fit test for the Rasch model. *Psychometrika, 38*, 123-140.

Angoff, W. H. (1982). Use of difficulty and discrimination indices for detecting item bias. In R. A. Berk (Ed.), *Handbook of methods for detecting item bias* (pp. 96-116). Baltimore, MD: Johns Hopkins University Press.

Arabie, P., Carroll, J. D., & DeSarbo, W. S. (1987). *Three-way scaling and clustering.* Newbury Park, CA: Sage.

Asante, M. K., & Gudykunst, W. B. (1989). *Handbook of international and intercultural communication.* Newbury Park, CA: Sage.

Barry, H. (1980). Descriptions and uses of the Human Relations Area Files. In H. C. Triandis & J. W. Berry (Eds.), *Handbook of cross-cultural psychology* (Vol. 2, pp. 445-478). Boston: Allyn & Bacon.

149

Bentler, P. M. (1992). *EQS structural equation program manual.* Los Angeles: BMDP Statistical Software.

Berk, R. A. (Ed.). (1982). *Handbook of methods for detecting item bias.* Baltimore, MD: Johns Hopkins University Press.

Berry, J. W. (1966). Temne and Eskimo perceptual skills. *International Journal of Psychology, 1,* 207-229.

Berry, J. W. (1976). *Human ecology and cognitive style: Comparative studies in cultural and psychological adaptation.* Beverly Hills, CA: Sage.

Berry, J. W., & Bennett, J. A. (1991). *Cree literacy: Cultural context and psychological consequences.* (Cross-Cultural Psychology Monographs No. 1). Tilburg, The Netherlands: Tilburg University Press.

Berry, J. W., & Dasen, P. R. (1974). *Culture and cognition: Readings in cross-cultural psychology.* London: Methuen.

Berry, J. W., Poortinga, Y. H., Segall, M. H., & Dasen, P. R. (1992). *Cross-cultural psychology: Research and applications.* Cambridge, UK: Cambridge University Press.

Berry, J. W., Van de Koppel, J. M. H., Sénéchal, C., Annis, R. C., Bahuchet, S., Cavalli-Sforza, L. L., & Witkin, H. A. (1986). *On the edge of the forest: Cultural adaptation and cognitive development in Central Africa.* Lisse, The Netherlands: Swets & Zeitlinger.

Best, D. L., & Williams, J. E. (1994). Masculinity/femininity in the self and ideal self descriptions of university students in fourteen countries. In A. Bouvy, F. J. R. van de Vijver, P. Boski, & P. Schmitz (Eds.), *Journeys into cross-cultural psychology* (pp. 297-308). Lisse, The Netherlands: Swets & Zeitlinger.

Bijnen, E. J., & Poortinga, Y. H. (1988). The questionable value of cross-cultural comparisons with the Eysenck Personality Questionnaire. *Journal of Cross-Cultural Psychology, 19,* 193-202.

Bijnen, E. J., Van der Net, T. Z., & Poortinga, Y. H. (1986). On cross-cultural comparative studies with the Eysenck Personality Questionnaire. *Journal of Cross-Cultural Psychology, 17,* 3-16.

Bochner, S. (1994). Cross-cultural differences in the self-concept. *Journal of Cross-Cultural Psychology, 25,* 273-283.

Bock, R. D. (1989). *The multilevel analysis of educational data.* San Diego, CA: Academic Press.

Bollen, K. J. (1989). *Structural equations with latent variables.* New York: John Wiley.

Bollen, K. J., & Long, J. S. (Eds.). (1993). *Testing structural equation models.* Newbury Park, CA: Sage.

Bond, L. (1993). Comments on O'Neill and McPeek's paper. In P. W. Holland & H. Wainer (Eds.), *Differential item functioning* (pp. 277-279). Hillsdale, NJ: Lawrence Erlbaum.

Bond, M. H. (1991). Chinese values and health: A cross-cultural examination. *Psychology and Health, 5,* 137-152.

Bontempo, R. (1993). Translation fidelity of psychological scales: An item response theory analysis of an individualism-collectivism scale. *Journal of Cross-Cultural Psychology, 24,* 149-166.

Borg, I. (1977). Geometric representation of individual differences. In J. C. Lingoes (Ed.), *Geometric representations of relational data* (pp. 609-656). Ann Arbor, MI: Mathesis.

Borg, I., & Lingoes, J. C. (1987). *Multidimensional similarity structure analysis.* New York: Springer.

Bracken, B. A., & Barona, A. (1991). State of the art procedures for translating, validating, and using psychoeducational tests in cross-cultural assessment. *School Psychology International, 12,* 119-132.

Bracken, B. A., & Fouad, N. (1987). Spanish translation and validation of the Bracken Basic Concept Scale. *School Psychology Review, 16,* 94-102.

Bravo, M., Woodbury, F. M., Canino, G. J., & Rubio-Stipec, M. (1993). The Spanish translation and cultural adaptation of the Diagnostic Interview Schedule for Children (DISC) in Puerto Rico. *Culture, Medicine, and Psychiatry, 17,* 329-344.

Brenner, S. O., & Bartell, R. (1984). The teacher stress process: A cross-cultural analysis. *Journal of Occupational Behaviour, 5,* 183-195.

Brislin, R. W. (1980). Translation and content analysis of oral and written material. In H. C. Triandis & J. W. Berry (Eds.), *Handbook of cross-cultural psychology* (Vol. 1, pp. 389-444). Boston: Allyn & Bacon.

Brislin, R. W. (1986). The wording and translation of research instruments. In W. J. Lonner & J. W. Berry (Eds.), *Field methods in cross-cultural research* (pp. 137- 164). Newbury Park, CA: Sage.

Brislin, R. W., Lonner, W. J., & Thorndike, R. (1973). *Cross-cultural research methods.* New York: John Wiley.

Bryk, A. S., & Raudenbush, S. W. (1992). *Hierarchical linear models: Applications and data analysis.* Newbury Park, CA: Sage.

Burton, E., & Burton, N. (1993). The effect of item screening on test scores and test characteristics. In P. W. Holland & H. Wainer (Eds.), *Differential item functioning* (pp. 321-335). Hillsdale, NJ: Lawrence Erlbaum.

Buss, D. (1989). Sex differences in human mate preferences: Evolutionary hypotheses tested in 37 cultures. *Behavioral and Brain Sciences, 12,* 1-49.

Byrne, B. M. (1989). *A primer of LISREL: Basic applications and programming for confirmatory factor analytic models.* New York: Springer.

Byrne, B. M. (1994). *Structural equation modelling with EQS and EQS/Windows: Basic concepts, applications, and programming.* Thousand Oaks, CA: Sage.

Byrne, B. M., Shavelson, R. J., & Muthén, B. (1989). Testing for the equivalence of factor covariance and mean structures: The issue of partial measurement invariance. *Psychological Bulletin, 105,* 456-466.

Camilli, G., & Shepard, L. N. (1994). *Methods for identifying biased test items.* Thousand Oaks, CA: Sage.

Campbell, D. T. (1986). Science's social system of validity-enhancing collective belief change and the problems of the social sciences. In D. W. Fiske & R. A. Shweder (Eds.), *Metatheory in social science* (pp. 108-135). Chicago: University of Chicago Press.

Campbell, D. T., & Fiske, D. W. (1959). Convergent and discriminant validation by the multitrait-multimethod matrix. *Psychological Bulletin, 56,* 81-105.

Campbell, D. T., & Stanley, J. C. (1966). *Experimental and quasi-experimental designs for research.* Chicago: Rand McNally.

Candell, G. L., & Hulin, C. L. (1986). Cross-language and cross-cultural comparisons in scale translations: Independent sources of information about item nonequivalence. *Journal of Cross-Cultural Psychology, 17,* 417-440.

Canter, D. (Ed.). (1985). *Facet theory: Approaches to social research.* New York: Springer.

Carroll, J. D., & Chang, J. J. (1970). Analysis of individual differences in multidimensional scaling via an *N*-way generalization of the "Eckart-Young" decomposition. *Psychometrika, 35,* 283-320.

Carroll, J. D., & Wish, M. (1974). Models and methods for three-way multidimensional scaling. In R. N. Shepard, A. K. Romney, & S. B. Nerlove (Eds.), *Contemporary developments in mathematical psychology* (pp. 57-105). San Francisco: Freeman.

Cattell, R. B. (1940). A culture-free intelligence test, I. *Journal of Educational Psychology, 31,* 176-199.

Cattell, R. B., & Cattell, A. K. S. (1963). *Culture Fair Intelligence Test.* Champaign, IL: Institute for Personality and Ability Testing.

Cheung, F. M. (1989). A review on the clinical applications of the Chinese MMPI. *Psychological Assessment, 3,* 230-237.

Cheung, F. M., Leung, K., Fan, R. M., Song, W. Z., Zhang, J. X., & Zhang, J. P. (1996). Development of the Chinese Personality Assessment Inventory. *Journal of Cross-Cultural Psychology, 27,* 181-199.

Chinese Culture Connection. (1987). Chinese values and the search for culture-free dimensions of culture. *Journal of Cross-Cultural Psychology, 18,* 143-164.

Church, A. T. (1987). Personality research in a non-Western setting: The Philippines. *Psychological Bulletin, 102,* 272-292.

Church, A. T., & Katigbak, M. S. (1989). Internal, external, and self-report structure of personality in a non-Western culture: An investigation of cross-language and cross-cultural generalizability. *Journal of Personality and Social Psychology, 57,* 857-872.

Cichetti, D. V., Showalter, D., & McCarthy, P. (1990). A computer program for calculating subject-by-subject kappa or weighted kappa coefficients. *Educational and Psychological Measurement, 50,* 153-158.

Clauser, B. E., Mazor, K. M., & Hambleton, R. K. (1994). The effects of score group width on the Mantel-Haenszel procedure. *Journal of Educational Measurement, 31,* 67-78.

Cleary, T. A., & Hilton, T. L. (1968). An investigation of item bias. *Educational and Psychological Measurement, 28,* 61-75.

Cohen, D., & Nisbett, R. E. (1994). Self-protection and the culture of honor: Explaining Southern violence. *Personality and Social Psychology Bulletin, 20,* 551-567.

Cohen, D., Nisbett, R. E., Bowdle, B. F., & Schwarz, N. (1995). *Insult, aggression, and the Southern culture of honor: An experimental ethnography.* Unpublished manuscript, University of Michigan.

Cohen, J. (1960). A coefficient of agreement for nominal scales. *Educational and Psychological Measurement, 20,* 37-46.

Cohen, J., & Cohen, P. (1975). *Applied multiple regression/correlation analysis for the behavioral sciences.* Hillsdale, NJ: Lawrence Erlbaum.

Commandeur, J. J. F. (1991). *Matching configurations.* Leiden, The Netherlands: University of Leiden.

Cook, T. D., & Campbell, D. T. (1979). *Quasi-experimentation. Design and analysis issues for field settings.* Chicago: Rand McNally.

Cortese, M., & Smyth, P. (1979). A note on the translation to Spanish of a measure of acculturation. *Hispanic Journal of Behavioral Sciences, 1,* 65-68.

Costello, R. M. (1987). Hispanic alcoholic treatment considerations. *Hispanic Journal of Behavioral Sciences, 9,* 83-89.

Cotter, P. R., Cohen, J., & Coulter, P. (1982). Race-of-interviewer effects in telephone interviews. *Public Opinion Quarterly, 46,* 278-284.

Cronbach, L. J. (1984). *Essentials of psychological testing* (4th ed.). New York: Harper & Row.

Cronbach, L. J., & Meehl, P. E. (1955). Construct validity in psychological tests. *Psychological Bulletin, 52,* 281-302.

Cronbach, L. J., & Snow, R. E. (1977). *Aptitudes and instructional methods.* New York: Irvington.

Cross, S. E. (1995). Self-construals, coping, and stress in cross-cultural adaptation. *Journal of Cross-Cultural Psychology, 26,* 673-697.

Cudeck, R., & Claassen, N. (1983). Structural equivalence of an intelligence test for two language groups. *South-African Journal of Psychology, 13,* 1-5.

Dana, R. H. (1993). *Multicultural assessment perspectives for professional psychology.* Boston: Allyn & Bacon.

Davison, M. L. (1983). *Multidimensional scaling.* New York: John Wiley.

De Groot, A., Koot, H. M., & Verhulst, F. C. (1994). Cross-cultural generalizability of the Child Behavior Checklist cross-informant syndromes. *Psychological Assessment, 6,* 225-230.

De Jong, M. J. (1987). *Herkomst en kansen. Allochtone en autochtone leerlingen tijdens de overgang van basis naar voortgezet onderwijs.* Lisse, The Netherlands: Swets & Zeitlinger.

De Raad, B. (1994). An expedition in search of a fifth universal factor: Key issues in the lexical approach. *European Journal of Personality, 8,* 229-250.

Deregowski, J. B., & Serpell, R. (1971). Performance on a sorting task: A cross-cultural experiment. *International Journal of Psychology, 6,* 273-281.

Devine, P. J., & Raju, N. S. (1982). Extent of overlap among four item bias methods. *Educational and Psychological Measurement, 42,* 1049-1066.

Diener, E., & Diener, M. (1995). Cross-cultural correlates of life satisfaction and self-esteem. *Journal of Personality and Social Psychology, 68,* 653-663.

Dijksterhuis, G. B., & Van Buuren, S. (1989). *PROCRUSTES-PC v2.0 user manual.* Utrecht, The Netherlands: OP&P Software.

Dogan, M., & Pelassy, D. (1990). *How to compare nations: Strategies in comparative politics* (2nd ed.). Chatham, NJ: Chatham House.

Dorans, N. J., & Holland, P. W. (1993). DIF detection and description: Mantel-Haenszel and standardization. In P. W. Holland & H. Wainer (Eds.), *Differential item functioning* (pp. 35-66). Hillsdale, NJ: Lawrence Erlbaum.

Dorans, N. J., & Kulick, E. (1986). Demonstrating the utility of the standardization approach to assessing unexpected differential item performance on the Scholastic Aptitude Test. *Journal of Educational Measurement, 23,* 355-368.

Drasgow, F., & Lissak, R. I. (1983). Modified parallel analysis: A procedure for examining the latent dimensionality of dichotomously scored item responses. *Journal of Applied Psychology, 68,* 363-373.

Dunnigan, T., McNall, M., & Mortimer, J. T. (1993). The problem of metaphorical nonequivalence in cross-cultural survey research: Comparing the mental health statuses of Hmong refugee and general population adolescents. *Journal of Cross-Cultural Psychology, 24,* 344-365.

Dyal, J. A. (1984). Cross-cultural research with the locus of control construct. In H. M. Lefcourt (Ed.), *Research with the locus of control construct* (Vol. 3, pp. 209-306). New York: Academic Press.

Earley, C. (1989). Social loafing and collectivism: A comparison of the United States and the People's Republic of China. *Administrative Science Quarterly, 34,* 565-581.

Ellis, B. B. (1990). Assessing intelligence cross-nationally: A case for differential item functioning detection. *Intelligence, 14,* 61-78.

Ellis, B. B., Becker, P., & Kimmel, H. D. (1993). An item response theory evaluation of an English version of the Trier Personality Inventory (TPI). *Journal of Cross-Cultural Psychology, 24,* 133-148.

Ellis, B. B., & Kimmel, H. D. (1992). Identification of unique cultural response patterns by means of item response theory. *Journal of Applied Psychology, 77,* 177-184.

Ellis, N. C., & Hennelly, R. A. (1980). A bilingual word-length effect: Implications for intelligence testing and the relative ease of mental calculation in Welsh and English. *British Journal of Psychology, 71,* 43-51.

Embretson, S. E. (1983). Construct validity: Construct representation versus nomothetic span. *Psychological Bulletin, 93,* 179-197.

Engelhard, G., Hansche, L., & Rutledge, K. E. (1990). Accuracy of bias review judges in identifying differential item functioning on teacher certification tests. *Applied Measurement in Education, 3,* 347-360.

Espe, H. (1985). A cross-cultural investigation of the graphic differential. *Journal of Psycholinguistic Research, 14,* 97-111.

Everitt, B. (1980). *Cluster analysis* (2nd ed.). London: Heinemann Educational Books.

Eysenck, H. J. (1986). Cross-cultural comparisons: The validity of assessment by indices of factor comparison. *Journal of Cross-Cultural Psychology, 17,* 506-515.

Eysenck, H. J., Barrett, P., & Eysenck, S. B. (1985). Indices of factor comparison for homologous and non-homologous personality scales in 24 different countries. *Personality and Individual Differences, 6,* 503-504.

Eysenck, H. J., & Eysenck, S. B. G. (1983). Recent advances in the cross-cultural study of personality. In J. N. Butcher & C. D. Spielberger (Eds.), *Advances in personality assessment* (Vol. 2, pp. 41-69). Hillsdale, NJ: Lawrence Erlbaum.

Farberow, L. (Ed.). (1975). *Suicide in different cultures.* Baltimore, MD: University Park Press.

Faucheux, C. (1976). Cross-cultural research in experimental social psychology. *European Journal of Social Psychology, 6,* 269-322.

Feldman, S. S., Rosenthal, D. A., Mont-Reynaud, R., Leung, K., & Lau, S. (1991). Ain't misbehavin': Adolescent values and family environments as correlates of misconduct in Australia, Hong Kong, and the United States. *Journal of Research on Adolescence, 1,* 109-134.

Fischer, G. H. (1993). Notes on the Mantel-Haenszel procedure and another chi-squared test for the assessment of *dif. Methodika, 7,* 88-100.

Forgas, J. P., & Bond, M. H. (1985). Central influences on the perception of interaction episodes. *Personality and Social Psychology Bulletin, 11,* 75-88.

Frijda, N., & Jahoda, G. (1966). On the scope and methods of cross-cultural research. *International Journal of Psychology, 1,* 109-127.

Geisinger, K. F. (1994). Cross-cultural normative assessment: Translation and adaptation issues influencing the normative interpretation of assessment instruments. *Psychological Assessment, 6,* 304-312.

Glass, G. V, & Hopkins, K. D. (1984). *Statistical methods in education and psychology* (2nd ed.). Englewood Cliffs, NJ: Prentice Hall.

Goldstein, H. (1987). *Multilevel models in educational and social research.* London: Griffin.

Greenfield, P. M. (1966). On culture and conservation. In J. S. Bruner, R. R. Olver, & P. M. Greenfield (Eds.), *Studies in cognitive growth* (pp. 225-256). New York: John Wiley.

Grob, A., Little, T. D., Wanner, B., Wearing, A. J., & Euronet. (1996). Adolescents' well-being and perceived control across fourteen sociocultural contexts. *Journal of Personality and Social Psychology, 71,* 785-795.

Guida, F. V., & Ludlow, L. H. (1989). A cross-cultural study of test anxiety. *Journal of Cross-Cultural Psychology, 20,* 178-190.

Guthrie, G. M., & Lonner, W. J. (1986). Assessment of personality and psychopathology. In W. J. Lonner & J. W. Berry (Eds.), *Field methods in cross-cultural research* (pp. 231-264). Newbury Park, CA: Sage.

Guttman, L. A. (1955). An outline of some new methodology for social research. *Public Opinion Quarterly, 19,* 395-404.

Hambleton, R. K. (1994). Guidelines for adapting educational and psychological tests: A progress report. *European Journal of Psychological Assessment (Bulletin of the International Test Commission), 10,* 229-244.

Hambleton, R. K., & Swaminathan H. (1985). *Item response theory: Principles and applications.* Dordrecht, The Netherlands: Kluwer.

Hambleton, R. K., Swaminathan, H., & Rogers, H. J. (1991). *Fundamentals of item response theory.* Newbury Park, CA: Sage.

Hamers, J. H. M., Sijtsma, K., & Ruijssenaars, A. J. J. M. (Eds.). (1993). *Learning potential assessment.* Lisse, The Netherlands: Swets & Zeitlinger.

Hammer, M. R. (1989). Intercultural communication competence. In M. K. Asante & W. B. Gudykunst (Eds.), *Handbook of international and intercultural communication* (pp. 247-260). Newbury Park, CA: Sage.

Hannover, B. (1995). Self-serving bias and self-satisfaction in East versus West German students. *Journal of Cross-Cultural Psychology, 26,* 176-188.

Harman, H. H. (1976). *Modern factor analysis* (3rd rev. ed.). Chicago: University of Chicago Press.

Hatfield, E., & Sprecher, S. (1995). Men's and women's preferences in marital partners in the United States, Russia, and Japan. *Journal of Cross-Cultural Psychology, 26,* 728-750.

Hattie, J. A. (1985). Methodology review: Assessing unidimensionality of tests and items. *Applied Psychological Measurement, 9,* 139-164.

Hays, W. L. (1994). *Statistics* (5th ed.). Orlando, FL: Harcourt Brace Jovanovich.

Hedges, L. V., & Olkin, I. (1985). *Statistical methods for meta-analysis.* Orlando, FL: Academic Press.

Helms-Lorenz, M., & van de Vijver, F. J. R. (1995). Cognitive assessment in education in a multicultural society. *European Journal of Psychological Assessment, 11*, 158-169.

Herrmann, D. J., & Raybeck, D. (1981). Similarities and differences in meaning in six cultures. *Journal of Cross-Cultural Psychology, 12*, 194-206.

Hess, R. D., Chang, C. M., & McDevitt, T. M. (1987). Cultural variations in family beliefs about children's performance in mathematics: Comparisons among People's Republic of China, Chinese-American, and Caucasian-American families. *Journal of Educational Psychology, 79*, 179-188.

Hierarchical Linear Modeling. (1992). *HLM*. Chicago: Scientific Software International.

Higbee, K. R., & Roberts, R. E. (1994). Reliability and validity of a brief measure of loneliness with Anglo-American and Mexican American adolescents. *Hispanic Journal of Behavioral Sciences, 16*, 459-474.

Ho, D. Y. F. (1996). Filial piety and its psychological consequences. In M. H. Bond (Ed.), *Handbook of Chinese psychology* (pp. 155-165). Hong Kong: Oxford University Press.

Hofstede, G. (1980). *Culture's consequences: International differences in work-related values.* Beverly Hills, CA: Sage.

Hofstede, G. (1983). Dimensions of national cultures in fifty countries and three regions. In J. B. Deregowski, S. Dziurawiec, & R. C. Annis (Eds.), *Expiscations in cross-cultural psychology* (pp. 335-355). Lisse, The Netherlands: Swets & Zeitlinger.

Holland, P. W., & Thayer, D. T. (1988). Differential item performance and the Mantel- Haenszel procedure. In H. Wainer & H. I. Braun (Eds.), *Test validity* (pp. 129-145). Hillsdale, NJ: Lawrence Erlbaum.

Holland, P. W., & Wainer, H. (Eds.). (1993). *Differential item functioning.* Hillsdale, NJ: Lawrence Erlbaum.

Homer, P. (1993). Transmission of human values: A cross-cultural investigation of generalization and reciprocal influence effects. *Genetic, Social, and General Psychology Monographs, 119*, 343-367.

Hoover, H. D., & Kolen, M. J. (1984). The reliability of six item bias indices. *Applied Psychological Measurement, 8*, 173-181.

Huang, C. D., Church, A. T., & Katigbak, M. S. (1995). *Identifying cultural differences in items and traits: Differential item functioning in the NEO Personality Inventory.* Manuscript submitted for publication.

Hui, C. H. (1984). *Individualism-collectivism: Theory, measurement, and its relation to reward allocation.* Unpublished doctoral dissertation, Department of Psychology, University of Illinois.

Hui, C. H., & Triandis, H. C. (1989). Effects of culture and response format on extreme response style. *Journal of Cross-Cultural Psychology, 20*, 296-309.

Hui, C. H., Triandis, H. C., & Yee, C. (1991). Cultural differences in reward allocation: Is collectivism the explanation? *British Journal of Social Psychology, 30*, 145-157.

Hulin, C. L. (1987). A psychometric theory of evaluations of item and scale translations: Fidelity across languages. *Journal of Cross-Cultural Psychology, 18*, 115-142.

Hunter, J. E., Schmidt, F. L., & Hunter, R. (1979). Differential validity of employment tests by race: A comprehensive review and analysis. *Psychological Bulletin, 86*, 721-735.

Ingelhart, R. (1977). *The silent revolution: Changing values and political styles among Western publics.* Princeton, NJ: Princeton University Press.

Inkeles, A., & Sasaki, M. (Eds.). (1996). *Comparing nations and cultures: Readings in a cross-disciplinary perspective.* London: Prentice Hall.

Ironson, G. H., & Subkoviak, M. J. (1979). A comparison of several methods of assessing item bias. *Journal of Educational Measurement, 16*, 209-225.

Irvine, J. T. (1978). Wolof "magical thinking": Culture and conservation revisited. *Journal of Cross-Cultural Psychology, 9*, 300-310.

Irvine, S. H. (1969). Factor analysis of African abilities and attainments: Constructs across cultures. *Psychological Bulletin, 71*, 20-32.

Irvine, S. H. (1979). The place of factor analysis in cross-cultural methodology and its contribution to cognitive theory. In L. Eckensberger, W. Lonner, & Y. H. Poortinga (Eds.), *Cross-cultural contributions to psychology* (pp. 300-341). Lisse, The Netherlands: Swets & Zeitlinger.

Irvine, S. H., & Carroll, W. K. (1980). Testing and assessment across cultures. In H. C. Triandis & J. W. Berry (Eds.), *Handbook of cross-cultural psychology* (Vol. 2, pp. 181-244). Boston: Allyn & Bacon.

Jensen, A. R. (1980). *Bias in mental testing.* New York: Free Press.

Jöreskog, K. G., & Sörbom, D. (1988). *LISREL 7: A guide to the program and applications.* Chicago: Scientific Software International.

Jöreskog, K. G., & Sörbom, D. (1993). *LISREL 8: Structural equation modeling with the SIMPLIS command language.* Chicago: Scientific Software International.

Kendall, I. M., Verster, M. A., & Von Mollendorf, J. W. (1988). Test performance of Blacks in South Africa. In S. H. Irvine & J. W. Berry (Eds.), *Human abilities in cultural context* (pp. 299-339). Cambridge, UK: Cambridge University Press.

Keppel, G. (1982). *Design and analysis: A researcher's handbook.* Englewood Cliffs, NJ: Prenctice Hall.

Kiers, H. A. L. (1990). *SCA: A program for simultaneous components analysis.* Groningen, The Netherlands: IEC ProGamma.

Kiers, H. A. L., & Ten Berge, J. M. F. (1989). Alternating least squares algorithms for simultaneous components analysis with equal component weight matrices for all populations. *Psychometrika, 54*, 467-473.

Kiers, H. A. L., & Ten Berge, J. M. F. (1994). Hierarchical relations between methods for simultaneous component analysis and a technique for rotation to a simple simultaneous structure. *British Journal of Mathematical and Statistical Psychology, 47,* 109-126.

Kim, S., & Cohen, A. S. (1991). *IRTDIF: A computer program for IRT differential item functioning analysis.* Madison: University of Wisconsin at Madison.

Kohn, M. L. (1987). Cross-national research as an analytical strategy: American Sociological Association, 1987 Presidential Address. *American Sociological Review, 52,* 713-731.

Kok, F. G. (1988). *Vraagpartijdigheid: Methodologische verkenningen.* Amsterdam: University of Amsterdam.

Kruskal, J. B., & Wish, M. (1978). *Multidimensional scaling.* Beverly Hills, CA: Sage.

Kuo, H. K., & Marsella, A. J. (1977). The meaning and measurement of Machiavellianism in Chinese and American college students. *Journal of Social Psychology, 101,* 165-173.

Lee, S. Y. (1990). Multilevel analysis of structural equation models. *Biometrika, 77,* 763-772.

Leung, K. (1987). Some determinants of reactions to procedural models for conflict resolution. *Journal of Personality and Social Psychology, 53,* 898-908.

Leung, K. (1989). Cross-cultural differences: Individual-level vs. culture-level analysis. *International Journal of Psychology, 24,* 703-719.

Leung, K., Au, Y., Fernandez-Dols, J. M., & Iwawaki, S. (1992). Preference for methods of conflict processing in two collectivist cultures. *International Journal of Psychology, 27,* 195-209.

Leung, K., & Bond, M. H. (1984). The impact of cultural collectivism on reward allocation. *Journal of Personality and Social Psychology, 47,* 793-804.

Leung, K., & Bond, M. H. (1989). On the empirical identification of dimensions for cross-cultural comparison. *Journal of Cross-Cultural Psychology, 20,* 133-151.

Leung, K., Bond, M. H., & Schwartz, S. H. (1995). How to explain cross-cultural differences: Values, valences, and expectancies? *Asian Journal of Psychology, 1,* 70-75.

Leung, K., & Drasgow, F. (1986). Relation between self-esteem and delinquent behavior in three ethnic groups: An application of item response theory. *Journal of Cross-Cultural Psychology, 17,* 151-167.

Leung, K., & Lind, E. A. (1986). Procedural justice and culture: Effects of culture, gender, and investigator status on procedural preferences. *Journal of Personality and Social Psychology, 50,* 1134-1140.

Leung, K., & Zhang, J. (1996). Systemic considerations: Factors facilitating and impeding the development of psychology in developing countries. *International Journal of Psychology, 30,* 693-706.

Lewis, C. (1993). A note on the value of including the studied item in the test score when analyzing test items for DIF. In P. W. Holland & H. Wainer (Eds.), *Differential item functioning* (pp. 317-319). Hillsdale, NJ: Lawrence Erlbaum.

Lidz, C. S. (1987). *Dynamic assessment. An interactional approach to evaluating learning potential.* New York: Guilford.

Lincoln, J. R., & Zeitz, G. (1980). Organizational properties from aggregate data: Separating individual and structural effects. *American Sociological Review, 45,* 391-408.

Linn, R. L. (1993). The use of differential item functioning statistics: A discussion of current practice and future implications. In P. W. Holland & H. Wainer (Eds.), *Differential item functioning* (pp. 349-364). Hillsdale, NJ: Lawrence Erlbaum.

Lipson, J. G., & Meleis, A. I. (1989). Methodological issues in research with immigrants. *Medical Anthropology, 12,* 103-115.

Little, T. D., & Lopez, D. F. (in press). Regularities in the development of children's causality beliefs about school performance across six sociocultural contexts. *Developmental Psychology.*

Little, T. D., Oettingen, G., Stetsenko, A., & Baltes, P. B. (1995). Children's action-control beliefs and school performance: How do American children compare with German and Russian children? *Journal of Personality and Social Psychology, 69,* 686-700.

Liu, H. C., Chou, P., Lin, K. N., Wang, S. J., Fuh, J. L., Lin, H. C., Liu, C. Y., Wu, G. S., Larson, E. B., White, L. R., Graves, A. B., & Teng, E. L. (1994). Assessing cognitive abilities and dementia in a predominantly illiterate population of older individuals in Kinmen. *Psychological Medicine, 24,* 763-770.

Long, S. (1983). *Covariance structure models: An introduction to LISREL.* Newbury Park, CA: Sage.

Longford, N. T. (1993). *VARCL.* Leicester, UK: De Montfort University.

Lonner, W. J., & Adamopoulos, J. (1997). Culture as antecedent to behavior. In J. W. Berry, Y. H. Poortinga, & J. Pandey (Eds.), *Handbook of cross-cultural psychology* (2nd ed., Vol. 1, pp. 43-83). Chicago: Allyn & Bacon.

Lonner, W. J., & Berry, J. W. (Eds.). (1986). *Field methods in cross-cultural research.* Beverly Hills, CA: Sage.

Lonner, W. J., & Ibrahim, F. A. (1996). Appraisal and assessment in cross-cultural counseling. In P. Pedersen, J. Draguns, W. Lonner, & J. Trimble (Eds.), *Counseling across cultures* (4th ed., pp. 293-322). Thousand Oaks, CA: Sage.

Lord, F. M. (1967). A paradox in the interpretation of group comparisons. *Psychological Bulletin, 68,* 304-305.

Lord, F. M. (1980). *Applications of item response theory to practical testing problems.* Hillsdale, NJ: Lawrence Erlbaum.

Lucio, E., Reyes-Lagunes, I., & Scott, R. L. (1994). MMPI-2 for Mexico: Translation and adaptation. _Journal of Personality Assessment, 63,_ 105-116.

Lynn, R. (1994). Sex differences in intelligence and brain size: A paradox resolved. _Personality and Individual Differences, 17,_ 257-271.

Markham, S. E. (1988). Pay-for-performance dilemma revisited: Empirical example of the importance of group effects. _Journal of Applied Psychology, 73,_ 172-180.

Marsh, H. W., & Byrne, B. M. (1993). Confirmatory factor analysis of multi-group-multimethod self-concept data: Between-group and within-group invariance constraints. _Multivariate Behavioral Research, 28,_ 313-349.

Mazor, K. M., Clauser, B. E., & Hambleton, R. K. (1994). Identification of nonuniform differential item functioning using a variation of the Mantel-Haenszel procedure. _Educational and Psychological Measurement, 54,_ 284-291.

McCrae, R. R., & Costa, P. T. (1985). Updating Norman's "adequacy taxonomy": Intelligence and personality dimensions in natural language and in questionnaires. _Journal of Personality and Social Psychology, 49,_ 710-721.

McCrae, R. R., Zonderman, A. B., Costa, P. T., Bond, M. H., & Paunonen, S. V. (1996). Evaluating replicability of factors in the revised NEO Personality Inventory: Confirmatory factor analysis versus Procrustes rotation. _Journal of Personality and Social Psychology, 70,_ 552-566.

McDonald, R. P. (1985). _Factor analysis and related methods._ Hillsdale, NJ: Lawrence Erlbaum.

Mellenbergh, G. J. (1982). Contingency table models for assessing item bias. _Journal of Educational Statistics, 7,_ 105-118.

Mellenbergh, G. J., Kelderman, H., Stijlen, J. G., & Zondag, E. (1979). Linear models for the analysis and construction of instruments in a facet design. _Psychological Bulletin, 86,_ 766-776.

Mercer, J. R. (1984). What is a racially and culturally nondiscriminatory test? In C. R. Reynolds & R. T. Brown (Eds.), _Perspectives on bias in mental testing_ (pp. 293-356). New York: Plenum.

Millsap, R. E., & Meredith, W. (1988). Component analysis in cross-sectional and longitudinal data. _Psychometrika, 53,_ 123-134.

Mislevy, R. J., & Bock, R. D. (1990). _BILOG 3: Item analysis and test scoring with binary logistic models._ Mooresville, IN: Scientific Software International.

Moghaddam, M. F. (1990). Modulative and generative orientations in psychology: Implications for psychology in the three worlds. _Journal of Social Issues, 46,_ 21-41.

Molenaar, I. W., & Fischer, G. H. (Eds.). (1995). _Rasch models: Foundations, recent developments, and applications._ New York: Springer.

Morris, M. W., Leung, K., & Sethi, S. (1995). _Person perception in the heat of conflict: Perceptions of opponents' traits and conflict resolution choices in two cultures._ Manuscript submitted for publication.

Multilevels Models Project. (1994). *MLn*. London: Multilevels Models.

Nandakumar, R. (1993). A FORTRAN 77 program for detecting differential item functioning through the Mantel-Haenszel statistic. *Educational and Psychological Measurement, 53,* 679-684.

Nenty, H. J., & Dinero, T. E. (1981). A cross-cultural analysis of the fairness of the Cattell Culture Fair Intelligence Test using the Rasch model. *Applied Psychological Measurement, 5,* 355-368.

Nisbett, R. E. (1993). Violence and U.S. regional culture. *American Psychologist, 48,* 441-449.

Nkaya, H. N., Huteau, M., & Bonnet, J. (1994). Retest effect on cognitive performance on the Raven-38 Matrices in France and in the Congo. *Perceptual and Motor Skills, 78,* 503-510.

Ombrédane, A., Robaye, F., & Plumail, H. (1956). Résultats d'une application répétée du matrix-couleur à une population de Noirs Congolais. *Bulletin, Centre d'Etudes et Recherches Psychotechniques, 6,* 129-147.

O'Neill, K. A., & McPeek, W. M. (1993). Item and test characteristics that are associated with differential item functioning. In P. W. Holland & H. Wainer (Eds.), *Differential item functioning* (pp. 255-276). Hillsdale, NJ: Lawrence Erlbaum.

Osgood, C. E., Suci, G. J., & Tannenbaum, P. H. (1957). *The measurement of meaning.* Urbana: University of Illinois Press.

Palisi, B. J., & Canning, C. (1983). Urbanism and social psychological well-being: A cross-cultural test of three theories. *Sociological Quarterly, 24,* 527-543.

Paniagua, F. A. (1994). *Assessing and treating culturally diverse groups: A practical guide.* Thousand Oaks, CA: Sage.

Paulhus, D. L., & Van Selst, M. (1990). The Spheres of Control Scale: 10 years of research. *Personality and Individual Differences, 11,* 1029-1036.

Pedhazur, E. J. (1982). *Multiple regression in behavioral research: Explanation and prediction* (2nd ed.). New York: Holt, Rinehart & Winston.

Petersen, N. S., & Novick, M. R. (1976). An evaluation of some models for culture-fair selection. *Journal of Educational Measurement, 13,* 3-29.

Peterson, M. F., Smith, P. B., Akande, A., Ayestaran, S., Bochner, S., Callan, V., Cho, N. G., Jesuino, J. C., D'Amorim, M., Francois, P., Hofmann, K., Koopman, P. L., Leung, K., Lim, T. K., Mortazavi, S., Munene, J., Radford, M., Ropo, A., Savage, G., Setiadi, B., Sinha, T. N., Sorenson, R., & Viedge, C. (1995). Role conflict, ambiguity, and overload: A 21-nation study. *Academy of Management Journal, 38,* 429-452.

Peterson, M. F., Smith, P. B., & Tayeb, M. H. (1993). Development and use of English versions of Japanese PM leadership measures in electronics plants. *Journal of Organizational Behavior, 14,* 251-267.

Plake, B. S. (1980). A comparison of a statistical and subjective procedure to ascertain item validity: One step in the test validation process. *Educational and Psychological Measurement, 40,* 397-404.

Poortinga, Y. H. (1989). Equivalence of cross-cultural data: An overview of basic issues. *International Journal of Psychology, 24,* 737-756.

Poortinga, Y. H. (1993). Cross-culturally invariant personality variables: A study in India and The Netherlands. In G. L. Van Heck, P. Bonaiuto, I. J. Deary, & W. Nowack (Eds.), *Personality psychology in Europe* (Vol. 4, pp. 105-153). Tilburg, The Netherlands: Tilburg University Press.

Poortinga, Y. H., & Malpass, R. S. (1986). Making inferences from cross-cultural data. In W. J. Lonner & J. W. Berry (Eds.), *Field methods in cross-cultural psychology* (pp. 17-46). Newbury Park, CA: Sage.

Poortinga, Y. H., & van de Vijver, F. J. R. (1987). Explaining cross-cultural differences: Bias analysis and beyond. *Journal of Cross-Cultural Psychology, 18,* 259-282.

Poortinga, Y. H., van de Vijver, F. J. R., Joe, R. C., & Van de Koppel, J. M. H. (1987). Peeling the onion called culture: A synopsis. In C. Kagitçibasi (Ed.), *Growth and progress in cross-cultural psychology* (pp. 22-34). Lisse, The Netherlands: Swets & Zeitlinger.

Poortinga, Y. H., & Van der Flier, H. (1988). The meaning of item bias in ability tests. In S. H. Irvine & J. W. Berry (Eds.), *Human abilities in cultural context* (pp. 166- 183). Cambridge, UK: Cambridge University Press.

Pretorius, T. B. (1993). The metric equivalence of the UCLA Loneliness Scale for a sample of South African students. *Educational and Psychological Measurement, 53,* 233-239.

Raju, N. S., Drasgow, F., & Slinde, J. A. (1993). An empirical comparison of the area methods, Lord's Chi-Square Test, and the Mantel-Haenszel Technique for assessing differential item functioning. *Educational and Psychological Measurement, 53,* 301- 314.

Raven, J. C. (1938). *Progressive matrices: A perceptual test of intelligence.* London: Lewis.

Reese, S. D., Danielson, W. A., Shoemaker, P. J., Chang, T., & Hsu, H.-L. (1986). Ethnicity-of-interviewer effects among Mexican-Americans and Anglos. *Public Opinion Quarterly, 50,* 563-572.

Reise, S. P., Widaman, K. F., & Pugh, R. H. (1993). Confirmatory factor analysis and item response theory: Two approaches for exploring measurement invariance. *Psychological Bulletin, 114,* 552-566.

Robinson, W. S. (1950). Ecological correlations and the behavior of individuals. *American Sociological Review, 15,* 351-357.

Rogers, H. J., & Hambleton, R. K. (1994). MH: A FORTRAN 77 program to compute the Mantel-Haenszel statistic for detecting differential item functioning. *Educational and Psychological Measurement, 54,* 101-104.

Rogers, H. J., & Swaminathan, H. (1993). A comparison of logistic regression and Mantel-Haenszel procedures for detecting differential item functioning. *Applied Psychological Measurement, 17,* 105-116.

Ross, C. E., & Mirowsky, J. (1984). Socially-desirable response and acquiescence in a cross-cultural survey of mental health. *Journal of Health and Social Behavior, 25,* 189-197.

Rudner, L. M., Getson, P. R., & Knight, D. L. (1980). A Monte Carlo comparison of seven biased item detection techniques. *Journal of Educational Measurement, 17,* 1-10.

Rummel, R. J. (1972). *The dimensions of nations.* Beverly Hills, CA: Sage.

Russell, J. A., Lewicka, M., & Niit, T. (1989). A cross-cultural study of a circumplex model of affect. *Journal of Personality and Social Psychology, 57,* 848-856.

Russell, J. A., & Sato, K. (1995). Comparing emotion words between languages. *Journal of Cross-Cultural Psychology, 26,* 384-391.

Samejima, F. (1969). Estimation of latent ability using a response pattern of graded scores. *Psychometrika Monographs, 34*(Suppl. 17).

Scheuneman, J. D. (1987). An experimental, exploratory study of causes of bias in test items. *Journal of Educational Measurement, 24,* 97-118.

Schmidt, F. L., & Hunter, J. E. (1977). Development of a general solution to the problem of validity generalization. *Journal of Applied Psychology, 62,* 529-540.

Schmidt, S. M., & Yeh, R. (1992). The structure of leader influence: A cross-national comparison. *Journal of Cross-Cultural Psychology, 23,* 251-264.

Schmitt, A. P., Holland, P. W., & Dorans, H. J. (1993). Evaluating hypotheses about differential item functioning. In P. W. Holland & H. Wainer (Eds.), *Differential item functioning* (pp. 281-315). Hillsdale, NJ: Lawrence Erlbaum.

Schwartz, S. H. (1992). Universals in the content and structure of values: Theoretical advances and empirical tests in 20 countries. In M. Zanna (Ed.), *Advances in experimental social psychology* (Vol. 25, pp. 1-65). Orlando, FL: Academic Press.

Schwartz, S. H. (1994). Studying human values. In A. Bouvy, F. J. R. van de Vijver, P. Boski, & P. Schmitz (Eds.), *Journeys into cross-cultural psychology* (pp. 239-255). Lisse, The Netherlands: Swets & Zeitlinger.

Schwartz, S. H., & Sagiv, L. (1995). Identifying culture-specifics in the content and structure of values. *Journal of Cross-Cultural Psychology, 26,* 92-116.

Schwarz, P. A. (1961). *Aptitude tests for use in developing nations.* Pittsburgh, PA: American Institute for Research.

Scribner, S., & Cole, M. (1981). *The psychology of literacy.* Cambridge, MA: Harvard University Press.

Serpell, R. (1979). How specific are perceptual skills? *British Journal of Psychology, 70,* 365-380.

Serpell, R. (1993). *The significance of schooling: Life-journeys in an African society.* Cambridge, UK: Cambridge University Press.

Shepard, L., Camilli, G., & Averill, M. (1981). Comparison of six procedures for detecting test item bias using both internal and external ability criteria. *Journal of Educational Statistics, 6,* 317-375.

Shye, S., Elizur, D., & Hoffman, M. (1994). *Introduction to facet theory: Content design and intrinsic data analysis in behavioral research.* Thousand Oaks, CA: Sage.

Sidanius, J., Pratto, F., & Rabinowitz, J. L. (1994). Gender, ethnic status, and ideological asymmetry. *Journal of Cross-Cultural Psychology, 25,* 194-216.

Sigel, I. E. (1988). Commentary: Cross-cultural studies of parental influence on children's achievement. *Human Development, 31,* 384-390.

Singer, E., & Presser, S. (1989). The interviewer. In E. Singer & S. Presser (Eds.), *Survey research methods* (pp. 245-246). Chicago: University of Chicago Press.

Singh, J. (1995). Now you see it, now you don't: A cautionary note on comparative cross-national analysis. *Journal of International Business Studies, 26,* 597-619.

Sinha, D. (1997). Indigenizing psychology. In J. W. Berry, Y. H. Poortinga, & J. Pandey (Eds.), *Handbook of cross-cultural psychology* (2nd ed., Vol. 1, pp. 131-169). Chicago: Allyn & Bacon.

Skaggs, G., & Lissitz, R. W. (1992). The consistency of detecting item bias across different test administrations: Implications of another failure. *Journal of Educational Measurement, 29,* 227-242.

Smith, C. S., Tisak, J., Bauman, T., & Green, E. (1991). Psychometric equivalence of a translated circadian rhythm questionnaire: Implications for between- and within-population assessments. *Journal of Applied Psychology, 76,* 628-636.

Smith, P. B., Dugan, S., & Trompenaars, F. (1996). National culture and the values of organizational employees. A dimensional analysis across 43 nations. *Journal of Cross-Cultural Psychology, 27,* 231-264.

Smith, P. B., & Peterson, M. F. (1988). *Leadership, organizations, and culture: An event management model.* London: Sage.

Sodowski, G. R., & Impara, J. (Eds.). (1996). *Multicultural assessment in counseling and clinical psychology.* Lincoln: University of Nebraska, Buros Institute of Mental Measurements.

Spencer, R. H. (1988). Translatability: Understandability and usability by others. *Computers in Human Behavior, 4,* 347-354.

Sperber, A. D., Devellis, R. F., & Boehlecke, B. (1994). Cross-cultural translation: Methodology and validation. *Journal of Cross-Cultural Psychology, 25,* 501-524.

Spielberger, C. D., Gorsuch, R. L., & Lushene, R. E. (1970). *State-Trait Anxiety Inventory.* Palo Alto, CA: Consulting Psychologists Press.

Sternberg, R. J. (1985). Implicit theories of intelligence, creativity, and wisdom. *Journal of Personality and Social Psychology, 49*, 607-627.

Sternberg, R. J., Conway, B. E., Ketron, J. L., & Bernstein, M. (1981). People's conception of intelligence. *Journal of Personality and Social Psychology, 41*, 37-55.

Stevenson, H. W., Stigler, J. W., Lee, S., Kitamura, S., Kimura, S., & Kato, T. (1986). Achievement in mathematics. In H. W. Stevenson, H. Azuma, & K. Hakuta (Eds.), *Child development and education in Japan* (pp. 201-216). New York: Freeman.

Stigler, J. W., Lee, S., & Stevenson, H. W. (1987). Mathematics classrooms in Japan, Taiwan, and the United States. *Child Development, 58*, 1272-1285.

Stigler, J. W., & Perry, M. (1988). Mathematics learning in Japanese, Chinese, and American classrooms. *New Directions for Child Development, 41*, 27-54.

Stocking, M. L., & Lord, F. M. (1983). Developing a common metric in item response theory. *Applied Psychological Measurement, 7*, 201-210.

Super, C. M. (1981). Behavior development in infancy. In R. H. Munroe, R. L. Munroe, & B. B. Whiting (Eds.), *Handbook of cross-cultural human development* (pp. 181- 270). New York: Garland STPM.

Super, C. M. (1983). Cultural variation in the meaning and uses of children's "intelligence." In J. B. Deregowski, S. Dziurawiec, & R. C. Annis (Eds.), *Expiscations in cross-cultural psychology* (pp. 199-212). Lisse, The Netherlands: Swets & Zeitlinger.

Tanzer, N. K., Gittler, G., & Ellis, B. B. (1995). Cross-cultural validation of item complexity in a LLTM-calibrated spatial ability test. *European Journal of Psychological Assessment, 11*, 170-183.

Tanzer, N. K., Gittler, G., & Sim, C. Q. E. (1994). A cross-cultural comparison of a Rasch calibrated spatial ability test between Austrian and Singaporean adolescents. In A. Bouvy, F. J. R. van de Vijver, P. Boski, & P. Schmitz (Eds.), *Journeys into cross-cultural psychology* (pp. 102-116). Lisse, The Netherlands: Swets & Zeitlinger.

Taylor, T. R., & Boeyens, J. C. (1991). The comparability of the scores of Blacks and Whites on the South African Personality Questionnaire: An exploratory study. *South-African Journal of Psychology, 21*, 1-11.

Ten Berge, J. M. F. (1986). Rotatie naar perfecte congruentie en de Multipele Groep Methode. *Nederlands Tijdschrift voor de Psychologie, 41*, 218-225.

Thissen, D., Steinberg, L., & Wainer, H. (1993). Detection of differential item func- tioning using the parameters of item response models. In P. W. Holland & H. Wainer (Eds.), *Differential item functioning* (pp. 67-113). Hillsdale, NJ: Lawrence Erlbaum.

Trafimow, D., Triandis, H. C., & Goto, S. G. (1991). Some tests of the distinction between the private self and the collective self. *Journal of Personality and Social Psychology, 60*, 649-655.

Triandis, H. C. (1992). Cross-cultural research in social psychology. In D. Grandberg & G. Sarup (Eds.), *Social judgment and intergroup relations: Essays in honor of Muzafer Sherif* (pp. 229-243). New York: Springer.

Triandis, H. C., & Berry, J. W. (Eds.). (1980). *Handbook of cross-cultural psychology: Methodology* (Vol. 2). Boston: Allyn & Bacon.

Tucker, L. R. (1951). *A method for synthesis of factor analysis studies* (Personnel Research Section Report No. 984). Washington, DC: Department of the Army.

Vallerand, R. J. (1989). Vers une méthodologie de validation trans-culturelle de questionnaires psychologiques: Implications pour la recherche en langue française. *Canadian Psychology, 30,* 662-680.

van de Vijver, F. J. R. (1988). Systematizing item content in test design. In R. Langeheine & J. Rost (Eds.), *Latent trait and latent class models* (pp. 291-307). New York: Plenum.

van de Vijver, F. J. R. (1991). *Inductive thinking across cultures: An empirical investigation.* Helmond, The Netherlands: WIBRO.

van de Vijver, F. J. R. (1994). Item bias: Where psychology and methodology meet. In A. Bouvy, F. J. R. van de Vijver, P. Boski, & P. Schmitz (Eds.), *Journeys into cross-cultural psychology* (pp. 111-126). Lisse, The Netherlands: Swets & Zeitlinger.

van de Vijver, F. J. R. (1996). *Meta-analysis of cross-cultural comparisons of cognitive test performance.* Manuscript submitted for publication.

van de Vijver, F. J. R., Daal, M., & Van Zonneveld, R. (1986). The trainability of abstract reasoning: A cross-cultural comparison. *International Journal of Psychology, 21,* 589-615.

van de Vijver, F. J. R., & Hambleton, R. K. (1996). Translating tests: Some practical guidelines. *European Psychologist, 1,* 89-99.

van de Vijver, F. J. R., & Harsveld, M. (1994). The incomplete equivalence of the paper-and-pencil and computerized version of the General Aptitude Test Battery. *Journal of Applied Psychology, 79,* 852-859.

van de Vijver, F. J. R., & Leung, K. (1997). Methods and data analysis of comparative research. In J. W. Berry, Y. H. Poortinga, & J. Pandey (Eds.), *Handbook of cross- cultural psychology* (2nd ed., Vol. 1, pp. 257-300). Chicago: Allyn & Bacon.

van de Vijver, F. J. R., & Lonner, W. J. (1995). A bibliometric analysis of the Journal of Cross-Cultural Psychology. *Journal of Cross-Cultural Psychology, 26,* 591-602.

van de Vijver, F. J. R., & Poortinga, Y. H. (1992). Testing in culturally heterogeneous populations: When are cultural loadings undesirable? *European Journal of Psychological Assessment, 8,* 17-24.

van de Vijver, F. J. R., & Poortinga, Y. H. (1994). Methodological issues in cross-cultural studies on parental rearing behavior and psychopathology. In C. Perris, W. A. Arrindell, & M. Eisemann (Eds.), *Parental rearing and psychopathology* (pp. 173-197). Chicester, UK: John Wiley.

van de Vijver, F. J. R., & Poortinga, Y. H. (1997). Towards an integrated analysis of bias in cross-cultural assessment. *European Journal of Psychological Assessment, 13,* 21-29.

van de Vijver, F. J. R., & Willemse, G. R. (1991). Are reaction time tasks better suited for ethnic minorities than paper-and-pencil tests? In N. Bleichrodt & P. J. D. Drenth (Eds.), *Contemporary issues in cross-cultural psychology* (pp. 450-464). Lisse, The Netherlands: Swets & Zeitlinger.

van de Vijver, F. J. R., Willemse, G. R., & Van de Rijt, B. A. M. (1993). Het testen van cognitieve vaardigheden van allochtone leerlingen. *De Psycholoog, 28,* 152-159.

Van den Wollenberg, A. L. (1988). Testing a latent trait model. In R.Langeheine & J. Rost (Eds.), *Latent trait and latent class models* (pp. 31-50). New York: Plenum.

Van der Flier, H. (1982). Deviant response patterns and comparability of test scores. *Journal of Cross-Cultural Psychology, 13,* 267-298.

Van der Flier, H., Mellenbergh, G. J., Adèr, H. J., & Wijn, M. (1984). An iterative item bias detection method. *Journal of Educational Measurement, 21,* 131-145.

Van Haaften, E. H., & van de Vijver, F. J. R. (1996). Psychological consequences of environmental degradation. *Journal of Health Psychology, 1.*

Vandenberg, S. G., & Hakstian, A. R. (1978). Cultural influences on cognition: A reanalysis of Vernon's data. *International Journal of Psychology, 13,* 251-279.

Vernon, P. A. (Ed.). (1987). *Speed of information-processing and intelligence.* Norwood, NJ: Ablex.

Watkins, D. (1989). The role of confirmatory factor analysis in cross-cultural research. *International Journal of Psychology, 24,* 685-701.

Werner, O., & Campbell, D. T. (1970). Translating, working through interpreters, and the problem of decentering. In R. Naroll & R. Cohen (Eds.), *A handbook of cultural anthropology* (pp. 398-419). New York: American Museum of Natural History.

Whiting, B. B. (1976). The problem of the packaged variable. In K. Riegel & J. Meacham (Eds.), *The developing individual in a changing world* (Vol. 1, pp. 303-309). The Hague: Mouton.

Williams, J. E., & Best, D. L. (1982). *Measuring sex stereotypes: A thirty-nation study.* Beverly Hills, CA: Sage.

Williams, J. E., & Best, D. L. (1990). *Measuring sex stereotypes: A multination study.* Newbury Park, CA: Sage.

Wilson, D., Cutts, J., Lees, I., Mapungwana, S., & Maunganidze, L. (1992). Psychometric properties of the Revised UCLA Loneliness Scale and two short-form measures of loneliness in Zimbabwe. *Journal of Personality Assessment, 59,* 72-81.

Wilson, M. (1988). Internal construct validity and reliability of a quality of school life instrument across nationality and school level. *Educational and Psychological Measurement, 48,* 995-1009.

Windle, M., Iwawaki, S., & Lerner, R. M. (1988). Cross-cultural comparability of temperament among Japanese and American preschool children. *International Journal of Psychology, 23,* 547-567.

Wrigley, C. S., & Neuhaus, J. O. (1955). The matching of two sets of factors. *American Psychologist, 10,* 418-419.

Yang, K. S., & Bond, M. H. (1990). Exploring implicit personality theories with indigenous or imported constructs: The Chinese case. *Journal of Personality and Social Psychology, 58,* 1087-1095.

Zegers, F. E., & Ten Berge, J. M. F. (1985). A family of association coefficients for metric scales. *Psychometrika, 50,* 17-24.

Zuckerman, M., Kuhlman, D. M., Thornquist, M., & Kiers, H. A. L. (1991). Five (or three) robust questionnaire scale factors of personality without culture. *Personality and Individual Differences, 12,* 929-941.

Author Index

Subject Index

About the Authors

Kwok Leung (Ph.D., University of Illinois) teaches in the Department of Psychology at the Chinese University of Hong Kong. He has published widely on cross-cultural psychology, organizational justice, and conflict resolution and has coedited several books, including *Innovations in Cross-Cultural Psychology* and *Progress in Asian Social Psychology*. He is currently an Associate Editor of the *Journal of Cross-Cultural Psychology* and the President-Elect of the Asian Association of Social Psychology.

Fons J. R. van de Vijver (Ph.D., Tilburg University) teaches in the Department of Psychology at the Tilburg University in The Netherlands. He has published widely on cross-cultural psychology and cognition, and he has coedited *Journeys Into Cross-Cultural Psychology*. He is currently an Associate Editor of the *Journal of Cross-Cultural Psychology*.